Pre chilli era | Post chilli era | White Curry
| Curry Renaissance |

CURRY HERITAGE OF THE TAMILS

From Ancient Roots to Modern Palates:
A brief history of Tamil Curry

RAVI MANIAM

DEDICATED TO MY WONDERFUL WIFE AND CHILDREN WHO DISPLAYED REMARKABLE PATIENCE WHILE I WAS WORKING ON THIS BOOK.

Curry Heritage of the Tamils – From Ancient Roots to Modern Palates: A brief history of Tamil Curry

Copyright © 2023 by Ravi Maniam

The purpose of this book is to provide accurate and trustworthy information on the subjects covered and to help bring the curry industry back to its former glory and prominence so that curry lovers can enjoy real, healthy and safe curry.

Please bear in mind that I am not a historian, and this book is not intended to be a comprehensive history volume. Instead, its primary focus revolves around the historical aspects related to curry.

All rights reserved. Printed in the United Kingdom.

For information contact :
www.thatscurry.com

ISBN: 978-1-84021-000-2
Publishers: Digitally Smart Media. England, UK
Author: Ravi Maniam ACMA, CGMA

First Edition: November 2023

10 9 8 7 6 5 4 3

The Chillies

Introduced by the Portuguese to the Tamils and that led to the
Curry Renaissance

The word "curry" originated from Tamil language and made its way into the English language through Portuguese influence in the 16th century, well before the establishment of the East India Company in the 17th century.

CONTENTS

PREFACE: THE CURRY CRISIS 1

INTRODUCTION: TAMILS' CURRY 8

CHAPTER 1: EXPLORING THE TAMIL LANGUAGE 16

CHAPTER 2: TACKLING THE CURRY CRISIS 35

CHAPTER 3: DICOVERING CURRY HERITAGE OF THE TAMILS 41

CHAPTER 4: INTRODUCING CURRY TO THE BRTISH INDIA 66

CHAPTER 5: PINNING DOWN THE DEFINITION OF CURRY 74

CHAPTER 6: RESPONDING TO THE CURRY CRISIS 94

CHAPTER 7: RECALLING HISTORY OF TAMILS & THEIR LANGUAGE. 104

CHAPTER 8: SEEKING VIKINGS IN THE CURRY LANDS 132

CHAPTER 9: GIVING THANKS TO THE NATURE – THAI PONGAL 144

CHAPTER 10: BRINGING BACK ANCIENT BEVERAGES 150

CHAPTER 11: DIFFERENT TYPES OF TASTES AND COMBINATION ... 150

CHAPTER 12: MAKING AUTHETIC TAMIL CURRY 150

APPENDIX 1: ANCIENT TAMIL LITERURE AND CURRY & PEPPER 195

APPENDIX 2: THE EUROPEANS WHO LEARNED TAMIL 206

APPENDIX 3: CULTURAL REMNANTS OF THE EUROPEANS 211

PREFACE

Curry Crisis

In recent years, the British Media has talked a lot about a curry crisis, the Great British Curry Crisis. This book discusses the crisis, the reasons why it arose, and about finding a solution to it.

But first, let me introduce myself, and my reasons for writing such a book.

I am a Tamil and a Londoner. Perhaps 'British Tamil' is the perfect way to describe me. I was born and brought up on a small islet off Sri Lanka, one that was previously colonised by the Portuguese. In fact, that islet was the first Portuguese - exclusive colony in that area, captured between 1499 and 1501 from the Jaffna Tamil Kingdom. The natives of these small islets were Tamils and Jaffna was the Portuguese name for 'Yarlpannam'.

Saravanai is my village in the islet which is the largest of all islets.

In fact, it is only because of who I am and where I was born, that I was able to talk to the Tamil scholars who helped me analyse ancient epic Tamil literature in which curry was referenced. I even learned the verses in which the word curry was used.

By the way, the Tamil language, as I will explain in chapter seven, is considered to be the world's oldest language! It is over five thousand years old, having made its first appearance in 3000 BCE. No surprise then that some of this literature dated back to the period before the Christian era. Today, armed with this knowledge, I can relay to the world the unique and untold history of curry.

The term "curry" is generally considered to have come from the Tamil word kari: which roughly means "sauce" (gravy), in Western usage, it indicates a dish seasoned with a mixture of ground spice. But before we go any further, I have a story to tell you. It is about how I started writing my book in 2015, three days before Christmas.

My eight-year-old son wanted a gift for Christmas. As I left for work that morning, I told him, "Listen. This afternoon, when I return from work, I want to take you to Currys, so make sure to be ready. I will text you soon as I leave work." Now I may need to explain to the reader, that in the United Kingdom, 'Currys' is not a restaurant but an electronic goods retailers. The ambiguity is what makes our little story.

That afternoon, as soon as I stopped the car in front of the driveway, he jumped in. He was very excited. To tease him, I told him, "At Currys, I will be ordering prawn curry and roti for dinner. What would you like for yourself? Fish cutlets and watila?" This was a reference to my son's favourite Tamil snack and dessert. But being English, of course, he knew we weren't going to a curry restaurant.

He looked at me and burst into laughter. He said, "You know what, Dad? Mum and I checked up on the name 'Currys' and learned that it is the surname of Henry Curry, the founder of the company who started it as a bicycle shop! But guess what, we also found out that the 'curry' we eat at home is a Tamil word."

I had heard that before – about the food, not the shop! – but never paid much attention to it. However, that day, because of the proud way my little Tamil boy said it, I decided to really look into it properly.

And straight away while we were in the car park of that Currys–PC World store in Ruislip, for at least twenty minutes checking the dictionary, a particular detail grabbed my attention and made me think.

Recall that the Oxford English Dictionary says that the Tamil word 'curry' came into the English language via Portuguese in the 16th century. Yet most curry lovers, link the term to the British and India.

But how can this be? India was established by the British, and that didn't happen until the 18th or 19th centuries. No, you see, the fact is that curry was around long before India even existed!

Here are some other interesting details that relate to curry.

FACT: The British East India Company was founded in the 17th century (31 December 1600). It was a private corporation formed to establish a British presence in the lucrative spice trade of the Indian subcontinent, which until then had been monopolised primarily by the Portuguese and the Dutch.

The British East India Company was the last European colonising force. As a matter of fact, it was active in the area at least 300 years after the Portuguese arrived in the region.

The Portuguese brought chillies and at least 130 other plants and vegetables, including wheat, tomato, potato, bean, cassava, pineapple, and pumpkin with them. This resulted in the development and Europeanisation of ancient curry with its authentic owners, the Tamils, in one of their two natural habitats.

I would even refer to this as the curry renaissance – a renaissance which began with the arrival of chillies, which are believed to have originated somewhere in Central or South America and were first cultivated in Mexico.

A few days after this, an article in the Financial Times caught my eye. It was headlined: 'The Great British Curry Crisis'. (January 8th, 2016.) Peter Backman, the managing director of a business named Horizons that monitors the British food industry, was quoted in the article written by Malcom Moore. What Backman said about curry was a matter of particular interest to me.

The British public is coming to an awareness that what

these curry houses are serving is not real Indian food." Likewise, towards the end of the article, Oli Khan, vice-president of the Bangladeshi Caterers Association (BCA), was quoted as stating, "This is now British curry. It is not Bangladeshi or Indian, itis British, and anybody can do it."

These two experts were saying the obvious, and especially Mr. Khan, and conceding to the reality that curry in Britain is of just one kind: it is now "British Curry".

As I read that article, I suddenly saw what might be the solution to the curry crisis. And I knew that if no one stepped in to solve the puzzle, the £4.5billion curry industry would die a natural death.

First of all, I realised that the confusion surrounding curry's authenticity and history needed to be eliminated. And secondly, I realised that as a Tamil, I was better positioned than almost anyone else, to relate to the public how Tamil curry, the true curry, came about.

Now you might be saying to yourself, "Okay, but there are other Tamils. Can't they tell this story too?" Well, actually no. Most Tamils in their other habitat, the Tamil Nadu state of India, would not have a clue about the Portuguese or Dutch influence on curry because they were not colonised by them.

In fact, these Tamil territories remained independent until the arrival of the British. The only Portuguese colony in the Indian subcontinent since 1510 was Goa, which was not a Tamil region. However, the Portuguese did establish numerous trading posts along the coastal areas known as the "curry zone" or 'Coromandel,' which were located in Tamil areas.

Because of this, the nearly 300-year-old story of modern curry can only really be told by the Tamils that were NOT part of British India, but part of British Ceylon, or, more specifically, the descendants of the Tamils on the islets and the former Tamil Kingdom of Jaffna. This is why I feel it is both my honour and my duty to explain to you, the reader, some of curry's historical background.

And I have another motivation too. I also feel that the curry industry needs help desperately. I honestly believe that the only way to save the curry industry is to tell curry lovers about its rich and 3000 years long history and explain where it comes from, who it actually belongs to, where it is going – all with indisputable evidence.

But first, a quick word about me. A few years ago, I moved to the UK and studied to become a qualified accountant (ACMA, CGMA) all while working in the financial district in the city of London as an IT consultant. Like many Tamils, I am also watching with concern about the curry crisis in the UK and naturally felt like doing something about it and so decided to write this book to help.

As far as I am aware, this is the first book from the 'other side'; one from those who actually own curry for these thousands of years. So I really hope you will both enjoy reading the book and appreciate and welcome my efforts to save the curry industry from what looks like impending disaster.

This book will discuss everything about the world's favourite spicy sauce. It will tell you the whole truth about curry, about both its ancient and modern history – and much more!

Ravi Maniam

ISLET OF KAYTS

This is the largest of all islets where world's first innovative curry powder of the Tamil and Portuguese came out 500 years ago.

INTRODUCTION

Tamils' Curry

It is said that the curry powder market of the world alone is now worth over two billion dollars. Two thousand million dollars! So, yes, curry is undoubtedly a very popular food in any part of the globe.

No wonder, a couple of years back, we saw on the news that a Russian billionaire had sent his private jet from Moscow to pick up a curry meal from his favourite restaurant in London. It is kind of impressive to think that curry could be so popular.

But it's not just Russians who like their spicy food. There's no doubt thatcurry is the favourite food in the UK too. However, here the industry it is facing many challenges and major media publications predict a bleak picture for it.

Why should that be?

The primary challenge regarding curry lies in its authenticity: What constitutes a 'real' curry, and who can claim ownership of it? These are questions both the public and the government seek to answer. Of course, there are thousands of glossy, beautifully presented curry recipe books out there. So many 'curry gurus' and 'experts' have written now about the topic and their books have sold in thousands if not millions. One book I read was boasting that a curry recipe has been developed in Britain– chicken tikka masala – and exported to India.

Amazingly, in 1747, Hannah Glasse in England published a recipe book, and a chicken curry recipe was there. Apparently, there was even a recipe written in the 14th century called "Forme of Cury".

But back to more recent accounts. Another book, simply called 'Curry', by Lizzie Collingham, was published in 2006. Lizzie painstakingly researched a lot but unfortunately limited her survey to India and wrongly concluded that curry is a product of India's long history of invasion. She failed to appreciate that the country nowadays called India was only established by the British, the last European colonial power in the region while under its direct administration beginning in 1858.

The point matters as the story of curry really starts in a part of the Indian subcontinent that definitely should not be mixed up with today's "India".

To make this point a different way, consider the Roman invasion of ancient Britain in 43 AD. It would be ridiculous to talk of the Roman invasion of the United Kingdom as the UK never existed back then.

Worse! None of these authors appear to have realised that the British East India Company Ltd also seized control –

at the time from the Dutch – of another country in 1796, which they called 'Ceylon'.

This all followed the Franco-Dutch war (1792 - 1802), when William V of the Netherlands fled to England from where he issued orders to governors of Dutch colonies to cede control of them to the British. The authorities in London didn't want to waste time and so, asked the East India Company's army based in Madras (Chennai) to take control of the Island's two areas colonised by the Dutch. This is how two countries became part of an empire run by a private limited company.

However, two years later, the British government recognised the island as a crown colony and Frederick North, second son of a British Prime Minister (Lord North, 1770 to 1782), was appointed as the first Governor of Ceylon in 1798. Hence, its administration separated from that carried out by the East India Company on the mainland. Two remaining kingdoms in the island, Wanni and Kandy, were captured in 1799 and 1815 respectively and a combined 'British Ceylon' was established in 1833.

Only much later did the Ceylon Independence Act of 1947 conferred dominion status on the colony, whereby Ceylon was recognised as an autonomous entity – with allegiance to the British crown!

Finally, in 1972, Ceylon became the Republic of Sri Lanka, all while maintaining its link with the British Commonwealth.

Anyway, we have now set the record clear about the importance of distinguishing Ceylon - today's Sri Lanka – and the rest of the sub-continent. We'll see why this matters in a moment for understanding the true story of curry.

Also note, after the end of the Franco-Dutch war, most of the former Dutch colonies were handed back by the

British EXCEPT Ceylon and South Africa.

Challenges facing curry

The word 'curry' is so much abused, and the wonderful food 'Curry' so often misrepresented that curry lovers today are easily taken for a ride by fakes and opportunists. The UK and the west are inundated with 'curry' from many different nations and this confuses the market as well as the governments. For example, to leave the spices to one side, for a moment – governments are confused about who to count as authentic curry experts - curry chefs – because there was no clear understanding of curry's geographical origins.

That's why, in the UK in recent years, the government has been under pressure from businesses for more visas for curry chefs arriving from many different nations. Such was the demand, there were even reports of 'people smugglers' bringing people as chefs into the country!

If restaurants don't have the right curry chef, let alone the right curry ingredients, then they won't win new customers.

Major media such as **The Financial Times, The Daily Telegraph, The Guardian, Channel 4 TV, ITV, SKY** and as recently as February 2022, **Aljazeera TV**, etc. predicted that in 10 years' time more than 50% of the UK's curry houses will be shut down due to falling numbers of customers and so business. They almost all use the headline, 'Curry Crisis'.

Some reports speculate that frozen curry meals, curry ready meals in the supermarket freezers and fridge shelves may be tastier than those being served in these curry houses which use curry paste for their curries which are now considered not only poor in taste but unhealthy too.

Some reporters even wrote that the curry houses target and serve 'fatty curries' to men high on lager while gym-going, health-conscious young people simply avoid curry houses. Of course, this increasingly negative image of curry restaurants and fast food outlets discourages families from visiting and enjoying the real thing.

Great British Curry Crisis

Sky - 2015	FT - 2016	Telegraph - 2017
[QR code]	[QR code]	[QR code]
Aljazeera - 2022	Guardian - 2023	ITV - 2023
[QR code]	[QR code]	[QR code]

Using your camera to scan and visit the relevant sites

And so, all of a sudden the curry industry talks about healthy curry. Michelin star winner, Aktar Islam, reckons health-conscious, gym-going youngsters see traditional curry dishes as too unhealthy. Another person in the industry says the industry should concentrate on healthy curry to woo back curry lovers to the 'Curry Restaurants'.

However, many people who picked up the notion of curry as if it was an orphan, are now ready to abandon it and walk away, unsure about what to do next and unable to answer the questions on authenticity.

A Family Business

There's another side to customers' concern about the authenticity of the curry: today the 'Indian Curry Houses' that operate as pockets of 'family businesses', long-serving curry to the nation, are disappearing fast at an alarming rate and it looks like it is going to continue in the same way too.

All of which is pointing to questions about who the curry actually belongs to. This is a natural question in a market where so many 'me too' varieties are now coming out.

Where the market started as Indian Curry, it is now inundated with many curries from different nations, most recently; the 'Vietnamese Curry'.

Other newcomers such as Nandos of South Africa are very successful partly because it says their flagship 'peri-peri' source is of Portuguese origin, clearly in an effort to demonstrate authenticity. (Actually in my opinion, 'peri-peri' is Dutch and not Portuguese, and later on in this book I will try to provide evidence to that effect.)

The simple story of curry coming from India is broken now with the curry industry losing its credibility – with both the government and the curry-loving public. In fact, it looks very much as if unless the facts and history of curry are told, the curry industry will eventually die and disappear! If not now, certainly sooner rather than later.

So, is curry an orphan without any authentic owners or history behind it? Well, not so fast. The curry that doesn't belong to any nation but has been called Indian curry, Bangladeshi curry, and lately 'British curry', is at least 3000 years old, a traditional heritage of the Tamils. Curry, for the Tamils, has been part of their traditional heritage for at least three millennia. It is the world's oldest food culture – just as it is linked to the world's oldest language: Tamil.

And that's why I've written this book: to help the curry and the curry food sector by giving a definite answer on authenticity by exploring about 3000 years of the history of curry with irrefutable evidence. Better still, the original version of the curry recipes from its natives, the Tamils, both 2500 year old pre-chilli era ones and nearly 500 years old post-chilli era ones are presented here too.

Let me explain again that what I call 'the post-chilli era' began with the arrival of Vasco da Gama bringing South American chilli to the Tamils. A member of the nightshade family, under the genus Capsicum, chilli peppers are native to the continent of South America where, as long ago as 7500 B.C., they used to grown as wild crops in New Mexico and Guatemala before being later domesticated by the natives.

However, sticking to the curry story, we will have to explore historical evidence to see the links between Tamils and their spices. We will also see how the curry of the Tamils is linked to those of other nations that are today marketing curry in the UK as well as in other western countries.

And let's start with the origin of the word 'curry'.

As per the Oxford English Dictionary, the word is derived from the Tamil Language. If you ask the BBC and Wikipedia, they will say the same too. Or you can just ask me, because I am a Tamil and a person who consumes curry at least twice a day, every day – so I should know what real curry is, shouldn't I?

Curry! at least twice a day, every day? You might wonder. But let me tell you, curry isn't limited to non-vegetarian cuisine. There's a wide array of vegetarian and vegan options, starting with the simple yet ancient Congee, which you'll soon discover. As you'll later learn, dishes like Biryani, Chapati, Naan, and Samosa, familiar to many in the West, do not belong to the Tamil curry tradition; they arrived from Arab or

Persian influences during the rule of the Mughal Islamic rulers in the northern Indian subcontinent.

Like many other Tamils, I have never used, nor will ever use, the so-called 'curry pastes', sauces or ready-to-eat frozen curry meals available in the supermarket. Because we don't know what is in that paste or sauce and we really don't want to know the ingredients that are in it.

Why? Because these supermarket products have many strange ingredients in them which should not be there, including preservatives and colouring agents. And if you don't know what ingredients are in the off-the-shelf curry paste that you buy, then you are risking your health.

Traditionally, Tamils avoid consuming curries that are more than two days old. However, in supermarkets, I often come across rice and curry displayed in open fridges with a long expiry date, indicating the use of preservatives that can compromise the dish's healthiness.

Okay, here, as U.S. President Joe Biden is famous for saying, is the deal; I will tell you all about the real, genuine curries the natives prepare and enjoy. Come with me to get into the nitty gritty details of at least 3000 years old traditional and 'authentic' curry-making practices of the Tamils. Because real curry making is easy, simple, and most importantly healthy. Oh, it is also inexpensive too.

But first, a bit about the Tamil people and their language. This is the topic of my first chapter.

CHAPTER 1

Exploring the Tamil Language

As I say, the Tamil Language is the world's oldest. Tamil civilisation is ancient, and its language is correspondingly rich in terms of resources and literature. The literature demonstrates that Curry and the Tamil people have a history that goes back at least 2200 years. But two recent events push the timeline of these events back to at least 3200 years. Examples include an Egyptian Mummy (details in Chapter Three) and a recent excavation activity in the Tamil region.

For example, as I am writing this, many Tamils all round the world are excited to read about a new archaeological excavation at Keelady, near Madurai in the Tamil Nadu state in Southern India, which is currently unearthing materials that confirm the existence of a civilisation near river Vaigai nearly 2600 years ago. This in turn would confirm the historical reality of the 'Sangam Period', the period of the history of ancient Tamil Nadu and Kerala (At that time, both regions were collectively known as Tamilzhakam, comprising the southern part of the subcontinent.) and parts of Sri Lanka (then known as Eelam) dating back to around the third century CE. It was named after the mythical and legendary Sangam academies of poets and scholars centred in the city of Madurai – but more about all this shortly.

Traditional Habitats of the Tamils

The oldest Tamil communities are those of southern India and the north and east of Sri Lanka. For thousands of years, the nativity of Tamils has been at the southern tip of the Indian subcontinent and the North and East of the island known traditionally as Eelam and now as a part of Sri Lanka.

Tamils had been living in the southern tip of the Indian subcontinent, known as 'Tamizhakam' and on the island of Sri Lanka, then known as 'Eelam' for more than 3000 years.

The Tamils of Tamizhakam, on the other side of the Palk Strait, became known as Indian Tamils after their habitat became part of British India (and now modern India since 1947) while the Tamils on the island, British Ceylon, became known as Ceylon Tamils – and after 1948, Sri Lankan Tamils.

In ancient times, there were three dynasties among the Tamils of the Indian Subcontinent: The Cheras, The Cholas, and The Pandiyas. Of these, the Cholas were the most powerful. They founded a Tamil empire across the sea in the 11th century, with a very powerful navy. Some of the Cheras became today's people of Kerala, whom the Portuguese

Vasco da Gama visited on 20 May 1498, while the rest settled in Tamil Nadu.

Today the Tamils of the Chera dynasty speak a newly branched-out language, called Malayalam, and after the 1947 independence from the UK, they live in the state of Kerala.

They are referred to as Malayalees and the Europeans were referring to them as Malabars. By the way, 'Malai' in Tamil means hill, and Kerala is full of hills and so also very green. Thus, "Malabars" literally means "People of the Highlands."

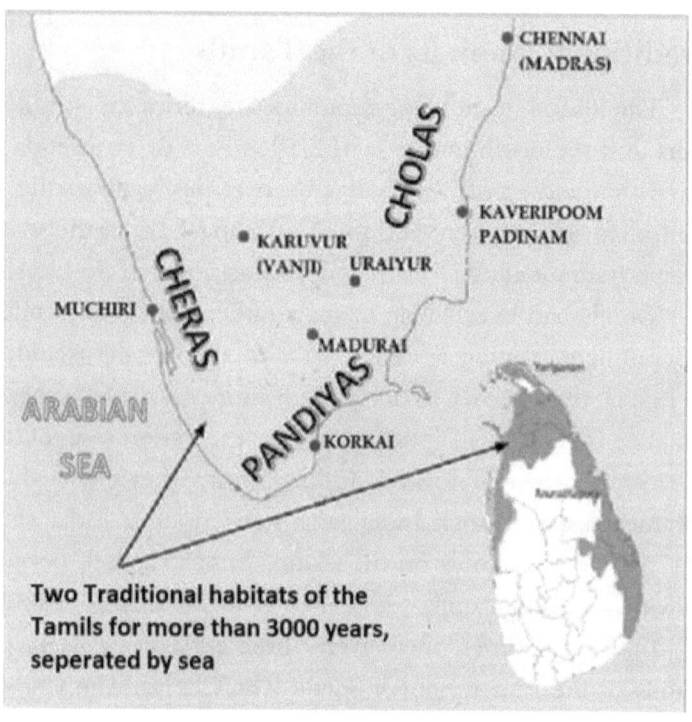

The **Cheras, Cholas** and **Pandiyas** *were three prominent ancient Tamil dynasties*

So, the traditional habitats of Tamils were the southern tip of the Indian subcontinent (known as Tamizhakam) and the island of Ceylon (Sri Lanka, referred to then as Eelam). These areas were known as the world's Spice Islands for thousands of years.

Many traders from other parts of the world travelled to them to acquire spice. The exchanges of Tamils with Arabs, Africans, Yavanas (of Greeks and Romans), Jews, Chinese, Malays, Javanese, Sumatrans, and many others are recorded vividly in ancient Tamil literature. (Please read more, in Appendix 1, of the ancient Tamil literature that refers to curry, spice, and foreign traders.)

The Two Tamil Traditional Habitats as of Today
The descendants of Cheras, one of the three dynasties continued to live in the southwestern coast but, in a separate state, Kerala

Arrival of the Portuguese - Vasco da Gama

After arriving in Kozhikode (Calicut) on the

southwestern coast of the Indian subcontinent in 1498, the Portuguese settled down in Kochi on the western coast.

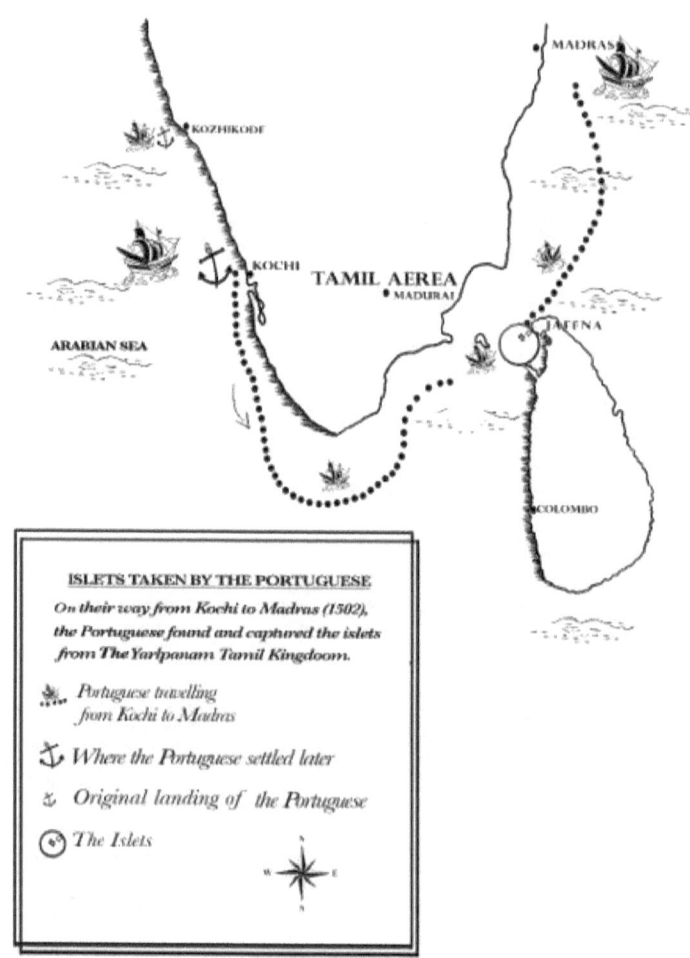

They immediately started exploring the area and eventually reached Madras (now Chennai) on the southeast coast in 1502.

The Yarlpanam (Jaffna) Tamil Kingdom, located in the northern most point of the island of Ceylon, included several islets. The Portuguese discovered these islets early in the 16th century (between 1499 and 1501) while travelling to Madras, conquered them, and settled there.

Later, the King of Yarlpaanam made a pact with the Portuguese under which he might continue ruling with the others, excluding the islets, in exchange for yearly tribute (of trained Elephants) to the Europeans.

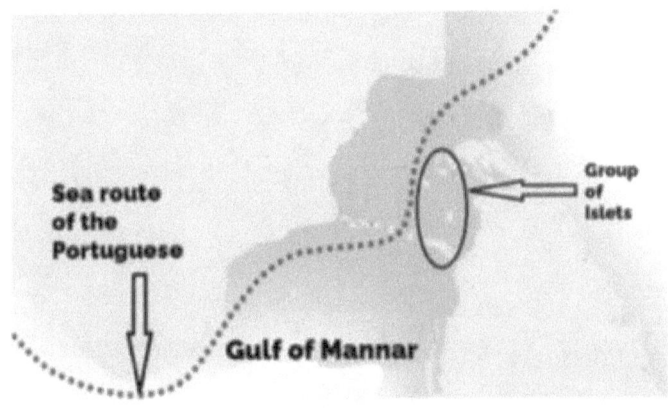

This group of islets was Portugal's first exclusive Tamil colony

According to historians, the Portuguese took control of these islets primarily in order to gain control of the Gulf of Mannar, where pearl fishing had long been an important economic activity. We will discuss about the pearls industry later.

The Portuguese then took control of the Jaffna Tamil Kingdom in 1616 following a brief battle that had been sparked by a quarrel during which the last Tamil King, Sankili

II, was killed.

Yarlpanam was referred to as Jaffna from this point onwards due to pronunciation concerns.

Statue of Sankili II, the last Tamil King of Jaffna

Likewise, the Portuguese arrived in the Southern part of the island in 1505 and started ruling it directly from 1574 onwards. But both regions were administered separately as there were two kingdoms, Wanni and Kandy, in between that were never captured.

It was only after the British captured the remaining two kingdoms, in 1799 and 1815 respectively, that all the colonies were combined as British Ceylon in 1833.

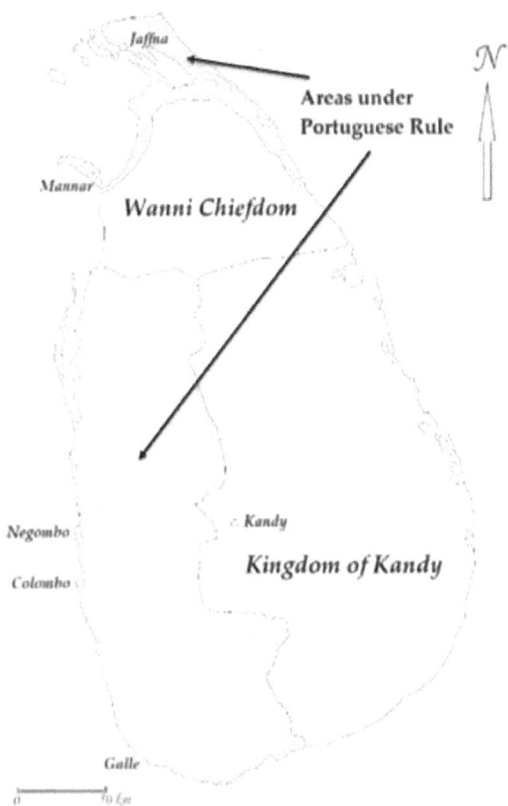

Ceylon - Early 17th Century

Talking about the islets mentioned above, I am actually from the largest one, and my home village, 'Saravanai', is even situated between two ancient Portuguese port towns – those of Cais and Chaddy. (Chaddy, means "shadow "in Arabic, suggests that the location was once an Arab trading post where an old mosque was located.). The Dutch who later on replaced the Portuguese changed the name Cais to Kayts, a name similar to that of a town in the Netherlands.

Today the name Kayts is still used. Another large village,

Leiden, now Velanai, is near to my village which again echoes the name of the city in the Netherlands.

Cheese lovers may know of a firm, yellow cumin spiced cheese made in the Netherlands called Leiden cheese (Leidse kaas in Dutch). The addition of cumin seeds gives the cheese a distinctive dry, tangy and spicy flavour, very unlike other Dutch cheeses, but the link between Leiden and spice is via the Tamils of my islet which was a former Dutch colony.

There is another islet called 'Delft', again the same name as that of a town in the Netherlands. The islet was renamed by the Dutch from its Portuguese name, 'Ilha das Vacas' which means literally, 'Island of the Cows'.

All over the region, many Portuguese and Dutch forts, some ruined, can still be seen. As can the descendants of the horses left behind by the Europeans, which still roam around the islets of Delft as wild animals, quietly reminding people of the European legacy.

Delft Island fort - First Portuguese fort in Tamil areas (later Dutch) - 500 years old and in ruins –

The ruined Portuguese fort in Cais (later Kayts) 500 years old

One Dutch fort, in Kayts is actually built in the middle of the sea. These forts and the churches built by the Europeans are now popular tourist destinations.

Fort Hammenheil (Dutch), in the middle of the sea, Kayts

Cumin has been used by Tamils since ancient times, often as a medicine, but the Portuguese introduced at least 130 new plants; vegetables and fruits, especially chilli which was cultivated and harvested in these islets.

Descendants of Chilli plants that Portuguese brought are still being cultivated in the islet villages

After capturing Jaffna and the peninsula, the Portuguese constructed a fort in 1618 in Jaffna. The Dutch took control of the fort in 1658 and expanded it. In 1796, it fell into the hands of the British, and it was maintained by a British garrison until 1948. This well-structured, pentagon-style fort served as the primary military stronghold not only in the Tamil regions during that period but later in British Ceylon.

It would not be an understatement to say that a renaissance of curry occurred just after the medieval time. It was with this, that what I call 'the post-chilli' era of curry began. And the development of curry continued further with the Dutch who replaced the Portuguese in the 17th century and in one particular islet that we now know as 'Curry Thuool'™ (Curry Powder) first came about.

Curry Thuool - Powder - is important. Simply put, there was no renaissance of curry without the new curry powder, 'Curry Thuool™', which became possible with the chilli, thanks to Columbus, who brought it to Europe from the

Caribbean, and Vasco Da Gama who took it from Europe to the Tamils who were until then using black pepper for their curries

.During the British colonial period of both India and Ceylon, some British traders also tried to replicate the recipe and came out with 'Madras Curry Powder', as it is called in Britain, but their mix didn't do particularly well, probably because they did not have the secret recipe that makes a perfect curry powder. Remember that the Curry Powder market is alone $2 billion worldwide and so still, today, there are many variants being produced by companies, coming out from non-Tamils, and then testing the market in vain.

Ancient Tamil way of powdering, using mortar and pestle

Efforts to make your own powder fare no well either. Curry lovers in the west always complain that curry recipes with confusing measurements, like two spoons of that, one spoon of this and half a spoon of that, and three-quarters of a spoon of this, fail, probably because of not knowing the correct ratios, as used in the "all in one" 'Curry Thuool™' (powder).

Base and rolling stones to make curry paste and Sambal – Ancient but still in use

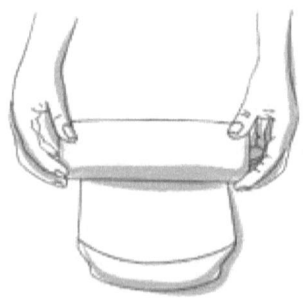

In fact, the ratio of ingredients, and the roasting times for individual ingredients, as well as the powdering methods that make a high-quality, perfect curry powder are closely guarded family secrets. At the same time, Curry Thuool (powder) was actually, a Tamil–European collaborative work, perhaps the very first one.

The Curry Renaissance

Please make no mistake; when I say, 'Curry Renaissance' it really was a period of new developments in the curry world, as it was not only chilli (and the resultant chilli powder) that the Portuguese brought with them but also many other vegetables that they introduced too: tomato, potato, sweet potato, cassava, pumpkin, leeks, beans, guava, cabbage, beetroot, red pepper, pineapple, peanuts, cashew nuts and papaya to name but a few. It was all this that completely changed the curry world of the Tamils.

Today, many of the Tamils living in their traditional habitats in Sri Lanka and India will naively refuse to accept that things like chilli, tomato, and potato are foreign vegetables introduced by the Europeans, notably because for them there is no curry without these.

This is why I term what happened following the introduction of Chillies and other vegetables as the "curry renaissance", while gently noting that the British, who were the last colonial power to settle in that region and arrived at least three hundred years after the Portuguese, who had colonised it first, played no part in it.

That's not to make snide points about the British! The point is to explain that the reason the authors of "Indian Curry" today are not discussing the curry renaissance is that they have no knowledge of it because they confine their writings and related research to the British and the nation they founded, "British India."

The Portuguese, Dutch, Danish, and French colonial powers that existed before the British are marginalised by them.

Keep in mind that they also disregarded or were unaware of the existence of "British Ceylon."

It's possible that the small island Ceylon, went unnoticed in the shadow of its larger neighbor, India.

The Original Curry Paste

Curry Paste started out as a pre-Chilli era mix, black pepper and herbs based, prepared daily, traditionally in base and rolling stones, freshly, for curry making.

And it's still being used today by the Tamils for some specific reasons and NOT for daily curry making. It is significant to note that, among Tamils, the mixture still largely retains the characteristics of the pre-Chilli era (almost no chillies in it).

However, what we have in the UK and elsewhere as 'curry paste' is a far cry from the stuff Tamils make and use, but is on the contrary, modified hugely with many strange ingredients including chillies and sugar and with preservatives that many Tamils think, make it unhealthy and also poor in taste.

Notice how these off-the-shelf, curry paste bottles are produced with warnings that say things like: "once opened, use within three days". Contrast with the real, Tamil curry powders, like dry-roasted Curry Thuool™ which will go for months, if not years.

Indeed, few Tamils buy or use curry paste from supermarkets but use their own mixes instead. Furthermore, whenever Tamils need it, the curry paste is made fresh, daily.

Sometimes it is used by new mothers, who are feeding babies, and to alleviate period-related pains, other times by people recovering from hospital surgery because, being herb based, it is considered to have protective and even curative properties. Would you believe that in the past, there was a unique curry paste made from special herbs that could expedite the delivery of a baby who was overdue?

Where authentic Tamil curry powder have a long shelf life, and are easy to work with, curry paste from supermarkets often must be used within three days once opened. To make matters worse, this leads some people (to try to avoid waste) to use the whole bottle for a curry that needs only a quarter or half of it!

Grinding stones for curry paste making

The Tamils still make curry paste using an antiquated method that involves grinding stones. Even in the West today, it is hard to find a Tamil kitchen without a granite base and rolling stones. One purpose of using grinding stones (base stone and rolling stone) is for making sambal which is extremely popular in Sri Lanka, Malaysia, and Indonesia.

Let me start by explaining a bit about geography. Recall that two areas of Ceylon (north and south), Malaysia (Malacca) and Indonesia were Portuguese colonies and later the same was Dutch colonies. Note too that, except for Goa which is not a Tamil region, there were no colonies of Portugal or the Netherlands in the Indian subcontinent.

During Dutch colonial times, Sambal, an Indonesian chilli sauce or paste, typically made from a mixture of a variety of chilli peppers with secondary ingredients such as shrimp paste, garlic, ginger, shallot, scallion, palm sugar, and lime juice. became popular but it is never too root in India as there was no Dutch colonisation but trading posts only.

For similar reasons, it is my opinion that Nando's peri-peri sauce, typically made using most ingredients like chilli peppers, lemon, vinegar, garlic, bay leaves, and oil, is also Dutch because South Africa was a Dutch colony at the same time as that of Malaysia, Indonesia, and two areas of Ceylon.

They introduced the usage of vinegar, wine, and even brandy in food and so in curry too. We will see later, a popular Dutch era 'Rich Cake' recipe made with dry fruits that are left to soak in brandy for weeks, if not months. At this point, I should also mention the 'Love Cake' that the Portuguese introduced too.

Hence the peri-peri sauce is basically a curry sauce introduced into South Africa by the Dutch taken there from its Tamil colony. While we talk about the Dutch, one more thing is worth discussing: donuts.

Vada(i) and Donuts

It is said that the Dutch settlers introduced donuts in their American colony of 'New Amsterdam' (the predecessor of New York) in 1621, and that later, by 1664, from New York, it came back to the Britain and Europe. So, it is clear they didn't take the recipe from the Netherlands.

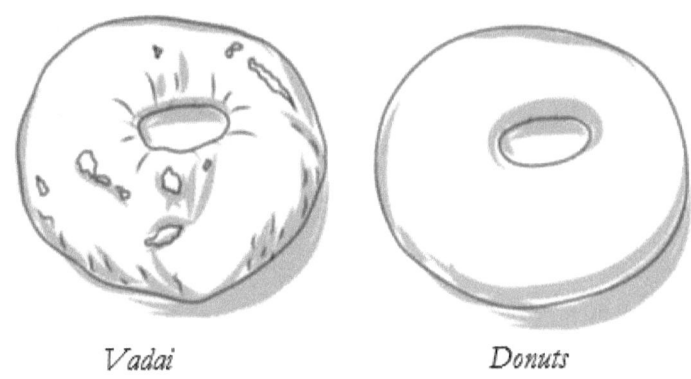

Vadai *Donuts*

However, the untold fact was that the Dutch East India Company (established on March 20, 1602) was active in the Tamil areas since 1608, and so do(ugh)nut was an impression of Vadai – traditionally made with urad dhal (black gram). According to food historian K. T. Achaya, Vadai (vada) was a staple food eaten by the ancient Tamils in the four hundred years from 100 BCE–300 CE.

Today it is a popular non-sweet snack, – doughnut shaped fried dumplings made with lentils – though there are sugar vada (sweet vada) versions available too. Even in the West, you hardly ever see a Tamil at a roadside stall (like Costa) sipping tea or coffee without a Vadai!

Sambal (or Sambol)

In Tamil traditions, a ground mixture of garlic, pepper, and salt is usually prepared as a side dish eaten with the cooked Palmyrah tree root tuber. Sambal is an extension of that. Sambal sauce is an integral part of the daily food of the Tamils in the island while among the Tamils in India, its cooked version, known as 'chutney' with some modifications, is used instead.

I am a huge fan of Coconut sambal and if I am given a

choice between, stone base grinder and a blade based electric grinder, to prepare the sambal, I will definitely go for the former as the taste from that can't be matched or beaten by the latter. (By the way, there are new developments in these electric grinders, and we now have base stone and rolling stone grinders but working on electricity. Remember that almost all blenders or grinders are working on blade concepts and so this is quite an innovative idea with an ancient tradition.)

Coconut Sambal is considered quite a delicacy among the native Tamils and there are at least six basic types (with many extended veg and non-veg varieties) are I would say that if you start using them, you will definitely say no to sauces that are with preservatives. We will see the recipes later.

Chapter 2

Tackling the Great British Curry Crisis

In a financial review, titled just that, "The Great British Curry Crisis", published on January 8, 2016, that surveyed the state of the £4.2b Curry Industry of the UK, the London Financial Times quoted a food management expert as saying that; "The British public is coming to an awareness that the curry served in those curry houses are not authentic." And the paper warned that it was this kind of public perception was leading the industry to lose out to newcomers such as Nandos, the South African multinational chain that specialises in Portuguese flame-grilled peri-peri style chicken, as they came to the British market with a clear authenticity statement.

So, the authenticity of the curry is an issue that has not been touched upon adequately yet, but increasingly the customers demand answers, and dodging this question is costing the industry immensely. Half-baked government responses, such as simply issuing visas to more curry chefs, or opening 'curry training centres', as offered by the government of David Cameron, have been in vain.

In the UK, curry has traditionally been marketed as Indian Curry and curry restaurants are popularly referred to as 'Indian Curry Houses'. However, the general branding 'Indian Curry' is increasingly unhelpful, when there are various rivals, such as Bangladeshi Curry, Pakistan Balti Curry, Sri Lankan Curry, Malaysian Curry, Singaporean Curry, Indonesian Curry, Korean Curry, Chinese Curry, Japanese Curry, Thai Red and Green Curry, Mauritian Curry, South African Curry, Caribbean Curry and lately Vietnamese Curry, that have now inundated the market. Add to which, as I say, there is now 'British Curry' too, adding further confusion to an already confusing situation.

Which is why, when organisations such as Pathak, the leading curry paste manufacturer in the UK, and Coco Ichibanya (a successful curry chain in Japan), boast that they are reaching out to India, the question is right there flying on our faces: 'so you are selling us something as coming from India but you say now you are going to introduce that same thing in India?' – it doesn't add up.

Staggeringly unsuccessful Corporate strategies on Curry

The curry industry is worth almost £4.5 billion in the UK alone and, as I say, much more globally, but there have been no successful corporate efforts here to match those achieved for pizza & pasta "from Italy", hamburgers "from

America", Kebabs "from Turkey", Tacos "from Mexico" and Nando's from "South Africa" (or maybe, from Portugal).

Even as the vegan food sector is said to have quadrupled between 2014 and 2022, the curry industry has not managed to keep up. The reason why it should have is that traditionally, curry primarily consists of simple vegetables, with meat being just an optional addition. However, in today's public perception, curry is often seen as linked with a meat dish and non-vegetarian cuisine.

The British Curry: Chicken Tikka Masala

The story behind this begins with a Scottish diner who expressed disappointment with their chicken curry, finding it too dry and spicy. The server brought the dish back to the kitchen, where a Pakistani cook added some double cream and a can of tomato soup to improve the dish. The dish was well received by the customer and quickly became popular, eventually becoming known as a British speciality.

However, repeating what's already been done feels like reinventing the wheel. Instead, let's examine the 'white curry' idea that originated from Tamil -European cuisine many centuries ago. It's important to recognise the origins of this dish and the unique cultural influences that shaped it.

By exploring these roots, we can truly understand and appreciate the dish for what it is rather than what it is not. Below, you will see the classification of curry and I am sure that will surprise you.

Who does CURRY belong to?

As I hope you are beginning to feel, this book introduces you to previously untold facts, backed with indisputable historical evidence. My next task is to try to establish which culinary tradition the curry you eat actually belongs to as well as explore different types of curries and curry-related food..

Curry Tradition of the Tamils.

Non-spicy (mainly vegan) curries are known as **white curries (milk curries)** and are suitable for the very old as well as the very young even babies aged six months onwards, Congees (or Kanji), Neechathanny, Mulligatawny, and hugely popular sambals, as well as some popular desserts including Wattlapaam and LumpPraias (Lump-Rice), a Tamil - Dutch luxury answer to Persian and Mohul (Arab) Biryani dish, are all Tamil curry traditions. However, many readers may not have even heard of white curries! We will revisit this topic, as well as the successes and failures of corporate efforts related to curry, later.

Okay, with this in mind, I will next discuss the watershed of curry's history with the introduction of chilli and of at least a hundred and thirty new vegetables or plants by the Portuguese colonists and Portugal's tremendous contribution to curry to which no credit had been given so far. Of course, some credit is also owed to the Dutch who followed the Portuguese.

All this took place in a period of over three hundred years, before the arrival of the British. So it is clear that anyone who talks about Indian Curry, alone, misses the history of curry development by the other Europeans (Portuguese, Dutch, Danish, and French) who were sailing to the Spice Islands and trading with the Tamils long before the arrival of the British and founded the country they called British India.

Let alone the fact invariably missed by other book authors on curry, that the British also established another country too and that was 'British Ceylon' —today's island of

Sri Lanka.

All this matters as to make sense of the development of the curry tradition of the Tamils over the last three thousand – or maybe more! – years, you have to understand that the Tamil people have been geographically scattered between two areas since time immemorial. One is the southern tip of the Indian subcontinent and the other is, mainly the north and east of the island of Ceylon known then as Eelam.

It is important to note too that while the Tamils in southern India were not subjected to any European rule – until the arrival of the British in the 18th century – the Tamils in Ceylon/Eelam had already been under the Europeans (Portuguese and Dutch) for nearly three hundred years before the arrival of the British. The British established a combined British Ceylon in 1833 by first taking the two separate parts of the island from the Dutch (1796) and then by capturing the Chiefdom of Wanni (1799) and the Kingdom of Kandy (1815).

Ceylon was different

Another point to note here was that the British decided to rule the island of Ceylon separately from that of India despite the two being separated by just eighteen nautical miles. By contrast, individual countries of today like Burma (Myanmar), Pakistan, and Bangladesh were part of British India.

Even the Andaman and Nicobar islands, which were 1400 nautical miles away from India, were brought directly under the Delhi administration and indeed are still part of India today.

Historians believe it was because of the three hundred years of European rule and the resultant cultural changes in the island that it was able to retain a very different character – and food culture – from that of British India.

Let's explore that next..

Chapter 3

Discovering the Curry Heritage of the Tamils

In this chapter, we will discover at least two thousand five hundred years of the 'pre-chilli era' as well as the next five hundred years of what I call the 'post-chilli era' curries.

First of all, let's start by the fact that, as we saw earlier, 'curry' is a Tamil word. In Sangam period literature, the word 'curry' is used to refer to pepper.

Today, however, curry refers to various side dishes like Kuzhampu (runny curry), Pirattal (dry Curry), lentils curry, spinach curry, and fish curry; all of which are usually eaten with rice. In English, such dishes are also called curry. It is a word that went from Tamil to English via Portuguese, in the 16th century century.

Along with 'curry', there are a few other food-related Tamil words too that can also be found in the English language. These are words like Poppadum, Mulligatawny, Rasam, Mango, and Congee. We will explore these terms and foods a bit more later. Other Tamil words that have found their way into English are Cash (Kaasu), Coir (Kayiru), Anicut (Anaicuttu), and Catamaran (Cattumaram).

The significance of the timing – the 16th century – means, these terms were being used by the English long before the establishment of the East India Company and before British trading activities and the colonization began in the Indian subcontinent. Remember that although the East India Company itself was registered in the 17th century on 31st December 1600,

the country India, as we know it today, was only formed by the company sometime between 18th and 19th centuries or legally in 1858 when the colony taken over by the British Crown.

The Spice Islands

The island of Ceylon and the Southern tip of the Indian sub-continent were the areas known as 'Spice Islands', places where spices were produced in plenty, chief amongst which was black pepper, the most precious spice of them all. This was so prized that it was called the 'King of Spices'.

In fact, right from the period before Christ (BC), and up until the start of the crusades at the beginning of the medieval period, Romans, Greeks, Jews, Chinese, Arabs, and African traders had all sailed to the Spice Islands for the seasonings as well as for their cotton, pearls, coir, and other treasures.

There's a curious story that links the Mummy of Pharaoh Ramses II and Black Pepper. Let me just share that with you now.

Ramses II, British Museum London

One of the greatest Pharaohs was Ramses II. He ruled Egypt from 1279 to 1212 BC. Long afterwards, by a special arrangement between France and Egypt, his embalmed body was taken to Paris and examined by scientists where it was found that black peppercorns had been stuffed in the nostrils, put there as part of the mummification ritual. This shows the significance and influence of the pepper, the King of the Spices.

It also clearly demonstrates the existence of an international spice trade between the Tamils and the Egyptians in the ancient world and that was about 3300 years ago. The Bible too has references to the spice trade, while the Roman trade with the Tamils was at its peak when they were ruling Egypt and they were bartering gold ornaments and wine for spices and pearls.

And it is the southern Indian subcontinent's Tamil region, where pepper is a native plant, that has long served as a hub for the international trade. It is revealing that many Roman coins have been unearthed in the Tamil area.

Remember, Cleopatra's pearls!

The industry of pearl fishing flourished throughout the Sangam era. The port city of Korkai in the Pandya empire served as the hub of the pearl trade. The Gulf of Mannar was well known for producing fine pearls, and a thriving pearl fishing industry developed there.

The ancient Tamil nation attracted international traders and visitors for its pearls, teak, coir, peacock feathers, ivory, spices, and incense.

The pearl fishing industry in particular, was well-established when Greek, Egyptian, Chinese, and Roman travellers and traders arrived at Korkai, the former location of the Pearl Fishery. Fisheries along the Pandyan coast are described in written sources from Greek and Egyptian explorers. And pearl from the Gulf of Mannar was the most costly sea product that the Roman Empire imported from the Tamil nation.

As early as 2300 BC, pearls were given as gifts to Chinese rulers, and in ancient Rome, pearl jewellery was regarded as the pinnacle of prestige.

"Pearls inferior to the Pandiayas sort are exported in great quantity from the marts of Apologas and Omana," the Periplus of the Erythraean Sea states. The inferior variety of pearls that the Tamils did not require for their use was in very great demand in the foreign markets.

Okay, now we understand the history behind the

narrative of Cleopatra's Pearl – how it came into being and why the Portuguese aimed to dominate this vital trade activity by securing all the strategic islets, including the islet where I was born, in the Gulf of Mannar.

But back to our spices. And black pepper itself has a long history dating back to 1200 BCE, when it was used as a form of payment and a gauge of personal wealth.

Some rulers used peppercorns as a form of tax payment and so it was also referred as 'Pepper-Tax' as well. In ancient Greece, when bartering was a common practice, pepper was used as currency and a sacred offering, as well as a seasoning. In addition to being used to pay taxes and ransoms, pepper was used to honour the gods.

A poem by the poet Imru' al-Qais, who was an Arabic poet of the sixth century CE, testifies to all this. The poet sings in memory of his girlfriend:

"The droppings of pigeons lay in her backyard. That too looks like precious black pepper to my eyes."

Arabian love poems like this underline to us the important historical fact that this ancient commodity of the Tamils went to the Arab countries.

Black Peppercorns – King of the Spices

The Post-Chilli Era

At the beginning of the medieval period, European Christians, at the request of the Pope in the Vatican, began what was calls a 'crusade' against the Ottoman Empire both for control of the holy place of Jerusalem, but also in the process for access to the spice islands.

As a result of the prolonged crusades, Arabian traders controlled the spice trade as they had exclusive access to the Mediterranean, the Red Sea, and the Arabian Sea. These were then the only trade routes for spices from Tamil areas to the West.

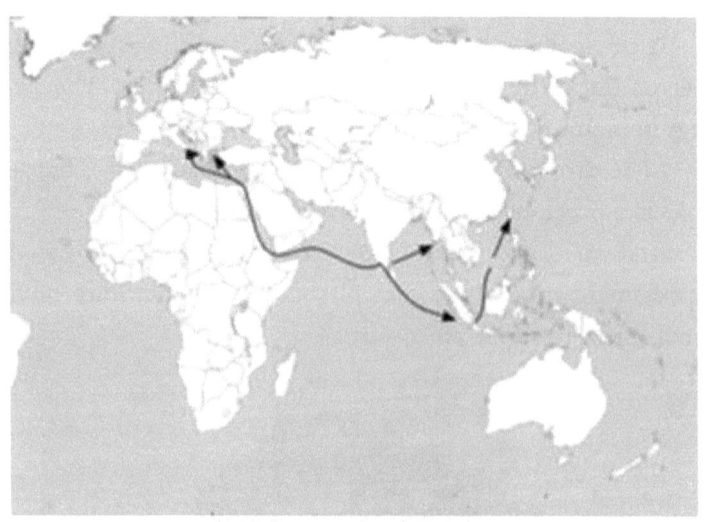

Ancient trade routes between Tamil areas and the rest

It was along these routes that pepper, cinnamon, cardamom, clove, ginger, incense, cotton, sandal wood, silk, coir, sea pearls, and oils moved – all part of a huge monopoly.

Towards the end of medieval times, the trade routes were firmly controlled by Muslim traders, while Alexandria and Italian cities like Venice and Genoa, were the major trading points for spices, once they had reached the Mediterranean. Arabian traders controlled the market, extorting high prices easily.

Pepper, therefore, had luxury status throughout medieval Europe, triggering a generalised fascination with spices and their exotic origins in the far-away lands of the Tamils. An individual's wealth was often measured by the amount of pepper in his inventory during the Middle Ages.

But it should be remembered that the Arabian traders also sold this spice to far eastern countries such as Maldives, Malacca, Sumatra, and Java (the last two are part of present-day Indonesia).

Their influence and wealth were so great that almost all of these countries' monarchs converted to Islam. Such was the huge power of black pepper!

Some of these countries were conquered at the beginning of the second millennium by the Tamil Chola dynasty. Emperor Rasa Rasan (King of Kings) had the first naval fleets in south East Asia. As a result, the Saivam, a sub-sect of Hinduism, spread to parts of these countries.

In the 18th century, Dutch colonialists discovered the ruined Prambanan temple hidden within a dense forest. This is the largest Hindu temple from ancient Java and has been designated as a UNESCO World Heritage Site. The temple prominently showcases the influence of the Cholas.

In 2012, while digging a drain, construction workers in Bali, Indonesia have discovered what is thought to be the biggest ancient Hindu temple ever found on this Indonesian island, archaeologists said.

(I will say a bit more about this later. For now, let us just note a point about Saivam as we will revisit 'Saiva meals' later.).

Prambanan Hindu temples, Indonesia

One result was the growing belief in Europe that the Arabs were funding 'the crusade' through the wealth acquired from their spice monopoly, which made the Europeans even more determined to break it.

Consequently, European traders, especially the Spanish and Portuguese, embarked on a quest to find an alternative route to the Spice Islands, marking the beginning of a new era in colonial history.

It was the Spanish that ventured out first.

Many authors have written about Christopher Columbus. Almost all of them relate him to the Spanish colonies and the new world, America. To my knowledge, no one, not a single author!, discusses Columbus' great contribution to curry though, and how he directly *contributed to the food sector.*

Well, this book will do him that honour.

The Voyages of Christopher Columbus

When Columbus set sail in 1492, with the sponsorship of the Spanish Monarch, and eventually arrived in the Caribbean, he strongly believed that he had reached the East Indies (India), in his search for a new route to the spice land of the Tamils. Ever since the islands of the Caribbean have been referred to as the West Indies.

Columbus and his crew had four voyages starting in 1492 followed by 1493, 1498, and 1502. However, it is only his second voyage in the following year in 1493 that comes within the scope of this book.

On this one, Colombus was accompanied by the royal physician, Diego Alvarez Chanca. The purpose of the expedition was to explore the herbs that the natives were using for ailments among them. The royal family must have heard of them from the crew of the first voyage and sent their own physician to explore this. The monarch could have anticipated the discovery of new medicines amongst those herbs.

Christopher Columbus

When the crew of Columbus returned in August 1494, collections of different seeds from the West Indies were packed in the luggage of Dr. Chanca. There were some important seeds too, which were to influence the food habits of the world. And amongst them were chilli seeds. This great contribution of Columbus has never been recognized to this date.

Remember that the potato, tomato, beetroot, pumpkin, pineapple, cassava, red pepper, beans, papaya, guava, Cashew and many more foods came to Europe from the new world. Given that millions died in Ireland when the potato crop failed in the 19th century, it is hard to imagine Europe today without potato chips, fries, wedges, and so on! But what about chilli?

Between 1494 and 1497, a handful of Christian monasteries in Spain, as well as in Portugal, grew chilli plants from the seeds brought in by Columbus' crew. In time, the chilli that was grown in the monasteries in Spain as well as in

Portugal, got the attention of the Portuguese royal family.

But that was later. In the meantime, Columbus was busy with his third and fourth voyages and into the gold rush of the New World. Had he known about the fortune chilli could have brought him, perhaps he would have focused on it instead, but history was to be written differently.

Relations with the Spanish crown became at one point so bad that he was stripped of his titles and summoned to the court while manacled in chains! He died a disappointed man, feeling he had been mistreated by his patron, King Ferdinand of Spain.

On the other hand, Vasco da Gama who sailed to the Spice Land of the Tamils with chilli was rewarded well and honoured by the Portuguese king Manuel I for his adventures in Asia.

The Portuguese and the chilli

Conventionally, history records Vasco da Gama reaching 'India' in May 1498 (as I say this is itself misleading as India never existed at that time, Calicut – or even Indian subcontinent - would be the correct word instead) and returning successfully with a precious cargo of black pepper and thereby opened a new route to the spice islands. Well, this was only one side of the story, what about the other side, the Tamils whom the Portuguese visited?

From the beginning, the Portuguese must have looked at it from a business perspective. Though they wanted to find a route to the Spice Islands and the Indian subcontinent, it was not just for the black pepper or other spices as many say.

Rather, as early as 1497, they must have figured out that in terms of spiciness, the chilli is far superior to black pepper and recognise that if positioned correctly, it could even replace it on the market.

On top of that, the original intention was to break the monopoly of the Arabs in the pepper trade.

And so, despite Columbus' failure to reach the original Spiceland, what he brought in from the new world was a matter of interest for the Portuguese. Which is why in 1497, explorer Vasco da Gama was commissioned by the Portuguese king to find a maritime route to the East.

Vasco Da Gama

It should be noted that the Atlantic slave trade began in 1444 AD, when Portuguese traders brought the first large number of slaves from Africa to Europe.

Hence, the west African coast was already familiar to the Portuguese sailors. What was not familiar was east of the south African tip that they referred to as the "Cape of Good Hope."

On May 20, 1498, Vasco da Gama arrived at Kappad (of Calicut), which was then part of the Kingdom of the Zamorin (Samuthiri Raja) of Calicut. Recall that this was part of the land of Cheras, one of the three ancient Tamil dynasties.

Vasco da Gama had an audience with the King but it was said that the King did not like the gifts he brought and so he was immediately expelled from the court.

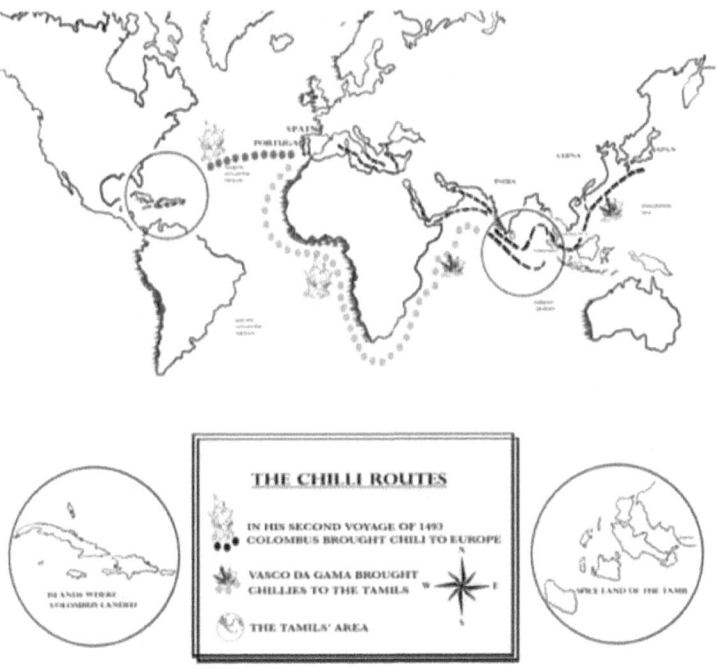

Historians say that on his way back to his ship the Muslim traders in the harbour area who resented the Portuguese as business rivals, attacked them and Vasco da

Gama lost many men before managing to return to the ship somehow and escape.

Vasco da Gama demonstrating chilli to King Zamorian

However, it was common sense that when a foreign trader arrives proposing new business, he would be treated well. What actually could have happened was that Vasco da Gama and his team must have presented the chilli to the king leading to the suspicion of the King and his courtiers that the new product would compete with their own 'flag ship' product, the black pepper.

And so Vasco da Gama and his team were shown the door and on their way to their ship they were attacked. This theory is supported as once the Portuguese left, it seems that some Muslim traders went on a rampage to attack Jewish settlers accusing them (wrongly) of bringing the Portuguese in to destroy their trade. (We will return to this later.

Anyway, the Portuguese were not going to give up on their mission so quickly, and so Vasco da Gama returned a few months later but this time with many ships, some fitted with dreadful cannons operated by well-trained men. They attacked and captured a place called Kochi, far away from the original landing place, and started cultivating and harvesting chilli there, before later on introducing the spice to the locals as well as also exporting it to other markets.

Getting to know their Chilli Peppers

In Tamil, there are two words concerning a fruit. If it is ripe it is called 'Pazham' and if it is unripe it is called 'Kaai'. An example of 'unripe' fruit is 'Mangkaai' (informally, 'Mangka') and this was introduced into the Portuguese language as 'Manga' (dropping the 'k') and from there took root in the English language as 'Mango'. (the 'a' at the end becoming an 'o'). The point though is that the word 'Mango' in English refers to... an unripe fruit.

Similarly, the chilli that was harvested in Koch(ch)i was

known then as 'Koch(ch)i-Kaai' (Green chilli of Kochchi). Because it was a new item to the Tamils, it was named after the place where it was cultivated first and came from.

Subsequently, it was transported to the nearby Ceylon Island and sold to other foreigners who came to purchase cinnamon, cardamom, and other goods, often after trading with the enemies of the Portuguese, the Zamorins, at the 'Kade,' the Tamil term for a shop or market.

So, these 'kade' areas were and still are known as 'Kochchi Kade', short for 'Kochchi-Kaai Kade' or 'the markets that sell unripe chilli from Kochchi'. Today, in Sri Lanka, many still refer to green chilli as 'Kochchi-Kaai'.

Almost five hundred years later, the coastal neighborhood area 'Kochchi Kade' thrives and remains popular in Sri Lanka's capital, Colombo, as well as in the nearby coastal town of Negombo. It serves as a polite reminder of the history of Chilli and the Portuguese connection.

Okay, we are getting near to dry Chilly and curry powder's innovative concept because the green chilli dried in the sun to become red chilli and this was then mixed with existing spices in a precise ratio and roasted (at a precise temperature, individually) before being pounded to get the perfect curry powder.

The Portuguese and Vijaya Nagara Empire

By the 1520s, there was a new drive by a more powerful Vijaya Nagara Empire, (Empire of the City of Vijaya) also called the Karnata Kingdom, into the southern part of the sub-continent, an expansion that put paid to ideas for Portuguese colonisation in the southern part of the sub-continent. Although the Portuguese were powerful in the sea, they opted to avoid confrontation on the land with an enemy whose forces greatly outnumbered the Europeans. They aimed to concentrate on their maritime strength, thus preventing other traders from entering for black pepper and securing a monopoly in the chilli trade.

It should also be noted that both powers aimed to contain the Islamic forces.

For the Vijaya Nagara Empire, the Moghul Islamic forces were pushing down from the north and so wanted to consolidate to be strong while, for the Portuguese, the confrontation was already in Europe - the Crusades. And so, having signed a treaty with the powerful Vijayanagara Empire rulers, the Portuguese maintained trading posts and moved out to Goa and the nearby island known then as Ceylon.

Goa, which was not a Tamil area, being the only colony of the Portuguese in the entire subcontinent and from that area, gave out on to a small area, present-day Mumbai (Bombay), as part of a dowry arrangement with King Charles II of England who had married the Portuguese princess, Catherine of Braganza.

As mentioned earlier, the Portuguese maintained trading posts throughout the southeastern coastal areas of the Tamils, many of which later became known as 'the Curry Zone' (Curry Mandalem) or 'Coromandel'.

They did, however, colonise many of the islets belonging to the Jaffna Tamil Kingdom, discussed earlier, the largest one of which was where I was born and brought up.

Portugal's goal in the Indian ocean, Bay of Bengal and the Arabian sea was to ensure their monopoly in the spice trade and also to market the chilli they brought in and were busy establishing several fortresses and commercial trading posts to this effect.

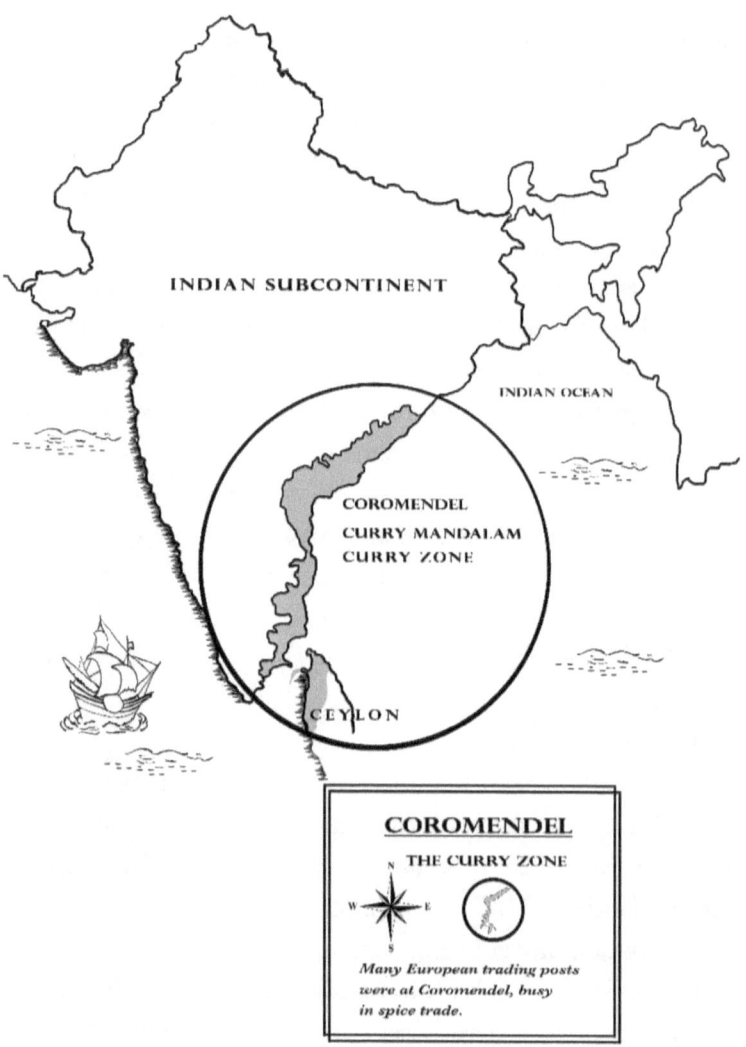

The Portuguese had superior weapons, and well-trained men and they used them to their advantage.

To achieve the monopoly, the Europeans had to stop two very important trading rivals, the Arabs and the Chinese. The former was distributing spices, mainly the precious black pepper, in Europe as well as in other Arab countries, and the far east countries, Malacca, Thailand, Java, and Sumatra.

The Chinese were doing the same kind of thing in mainland China, Korea, Japan, Laos, Vietnam, and Cambodia.

While in the Kochi area the Portuguese saw the Chinese ships passing them and trading with their enemies, the Zamorins. They observed that Arabs ships with spices passed them to go to countries in the far east such as Malacca, Java, Sumitra, and also the Maldives.

The Porta de Santiago, a small gate house, is the only remaining part of the Portuguese fortress still standing in Malacca, Malaysia.

In 1511, the Portuguese acted swiftly, capturing Malacca (Malaysia) in an effort to block Chinese trade with the spice-producing lands. The Chinese were accessing these regions by sailing through the Malacca Strait.

The Portuguese received assistance in this endeavor from Spain, which had earlier colonized the Philippines. After numerous direct battles with the Chinese, the Portuguese went on to establish their own colony in Macau in 1557. This ensured that, from that point onward, they had control over the Far East and the Chinese spice trade, with an emphasis on Chilli rather than pepper.

This history is the reason we now have Chinese Curry and Malaysian Curry! Interestingly, China has become the world's largest producer of Chilli peppers, a commodity originally introduced by the Portuguese.

But remember that the Chinese had pre-chilli era link with the Tamils. Note that I have discussed elsewhere in this book of Chinese excavation activities of 2017 in 'Allaipiddy', a coastal village in my islet.

The Portuguese also established their presence in the Persian Gulf and the Arabian Peninsula, with the participation of two sons of Vasco da Gama. This shattered the Arabs' long-standing monopoly on the spice trade. The Arabian influence in the black pepper trade and Tamil curry predates the Chilli era, while the dish known as 'Biryani,' developed from the ancient Tamil delicacy 'Uhoon Soru' (Meat Rice), is also a pre-Chilli era delicacy.

Subsequently, the Portuguese expanded their influence along the East African Coast and colonized Mozambique. This contributed to the development of the dish known today as 'Ethiopian Curry'.

Let me briefly explain the link. The story dates back to 1529 when Ethiopia was invaded by the Somali Imam, Ahmed Gragn. Emperor Lebna Dengel first sought Portuguese assistance in 1520 to help defeat the Adal Sultanate.

The 'Berbere,' a special curry powder widely used in Ethiopia, particularly in the popular dish 'Dorowat' (Ethiopian Berbere Chicken Curry), is a result of Portuguese influence in the region. The concept of 'berbere' likely passed from the Portuguese to their first exclusive Tamil colony, where the world's first Tamil Chilli powder was developed.

The Portuguese first arrived in Thailand (then Siam) in 1511 – over five hundred years ago – and signed a treaty with the Thai king, allowing Portuguese settlers to trade freely. Thailand was not colonized by the Portuguese, but their influence, particularly from Portuguese-Tamil curry, led to the creation of Thai red and green curries. Both red and green curries are indeed post-chilli era curries.

Many Thai curries feature coconut milk, which imparts a distinctive flavor similar to the 'white curries' of the Tamils in the Portuguese colonies in the northern part of the island of Ceylon.

Japanese Curry

The first Portuguese (and incidentally, Western) landing on Japanese soil appears to have occurred in 1543 when a group of Portuguese merchants, traveling aboard a trade junk toward China, was blown off course and found themselves on the island of Tanegashima.

Following this event, trade commenced between Portugal, Portuguese Tamil regions, Portuguese African regions, Portuguese Arab regions, Portuguese Malacca, Portuguese Macau, Portuguese Indonesia (East Timor), Thailand, China, and Japan.

All of this means that, thanks to the Tamils, the Portuguese, and the curry renaissance, we now have Japanese, Chinese, and Thai curries.

It's important to note that these developments all occurred in the post-chilli era. We will explore the pre-chilli era connections shortly.

In a later chapter, we will delve into the reasons behind the growing popularity of Thai and Japanese curries in the

West, including the UK.

The Portuguese were right about chilli.

The Portuguese, particularly Vasco da Gama and his crew, were proven right. Thanks to their efforts, Chilli was introduced to regions where black pepper was the primary spice, eventually leading to the dethronement of black pepper, which had long been considered the king of spices.

The spread of chilli throughout Asia, especially among the Tamils, was swift. The Tamils and their curry readily adapted their culinary preferences, transitioning from black pepper to chilli over time.

Today, curry can be prepared without pepper, but not without chilli. It's worth noting that, for its distinct flavor, one or two green Chillies are often added to curries in addition to the red chilli-based curry powder.

Over the next five hundred years, chilli became increasingly popular throughout the world. Of course, today, black pepper can still be found on dinner tables. It can't, however, return to the place that it was enjoying once, just because of the chilli that was brought into Europe by Columbus.

As of today, India is the second largest producer of chilli after China.

To illustrate the substitution of black pepper with chili, the Portuguese turned to the curry of the Tamils, and the Tamil chefs, from the colonies of islets off Jaffna.

Another noteworthy point involves a small French colony in the Tamil region. By the end of the 17th century, the French had established a strong presence in Pondicherry (now Puducherry), located along the Coromandel Coast in Tamil Nadu. Pondicherry's connection to Vietnam, Cambodia, and Laos (French Indochina), all of which were under French rule, particularly in terms of food tradition, is significant.

The French Indochina colonies were overseen by the French Governors in Pondicherry (now Puducherry), leading to a significant exchange of people. Many Tamils moved to those colonies, and vice versa, for trade and even as warriors.

This led to the evolution of Vietnamese Curry. Tamil-Vietnamese cuisine is an essential component of both Pondicherry Cuisine and Vietnamese cuisine. So, if you encounter a menu offering Vietnamese Curry, you will now understand the history behind it and its connection to Tamil curry. It was, however, a pre-chilli era curry that underwent further development in Vietnam.

I have already indicated that there are two natural habitats of Tamils: one in south India and the other in Sri Lanka. Pudicherry was a French colony and is now a small union territory (like Indian Capital Delhi, a union territory) within India but not within Tamil Nadu state but surrounded by it except on one side which is the sea. However, for the purpose of this book on curry, let us consider this as part of the southern Indian Tamil habitat.

Uhoon-Soru (Meat Rice) of the Tamils and Arabs' Biryani

Many authors believe and have written that Biriyani is an Arab delicacy that originated in Persia (Iran) before later coming into the sub-continent with the Mughal rulers. However, this is not correct. on the contrary, biryani is an Arab name for an ancient Tamil dish.

The ancient Tamil literature talks of a dish called 'Uhoon-Soru' — 'Meat Rice'– too, made with rice, cow ghee, honey, pepper, turmeric, coriander, ginger and meat.

'Purananuru' (புறநானூறு), the oldest compilation of poems in the world (composed of Tamil poems of various authors between 200 BCE to 200 CE) contains a verse, number 33, that describes the Chola King, NalanKilli, serving 'Uhoon (meat) and Soru (rice) on the battlefield to the soldiers who defeated the Pandiya king and captured his fort.

'Purananuru' poem 382 says, a poet who, affected by famine, sang in praise of King Nallangkilli following his battle victory. In recognition of his efforts, which pleased the king, the poet was offered UhoonSoru, a dish made with rice, ghee, turmeric, ginger, and ram meat.

Another verse, number 113, describes the killing of King Vel Paari by the treachery of the Chera, Chola, and Pandiya kings. Vel Paari was a great philanthropist and was known to give to anyone who came to him and ask for alms. And so, later, the poet Kapilar weeps:

"Who will feed us 'Uhoon-Soru' made with ram meat and rice? He who also gives us honey with great love is no more and I am leaving this hill with great sorrow."

* (Kapilar (Tamil: கபிலர்) was the most prolific Tamil poet of the Sangam era.)

This 'Uhoon-Soru' is mentioned numerous times in Pura-Nanooru and Madurai-Kanchi, both of which are ancient Tamil literature. Verse 33 was compiled around 115 BCE, while the Mughals invaded the northern part of the subcontinent by 1526, which was at least 1600 years later. The point here is that the Arab traders, who came to the Tamils for spices, not only enjoyed 'Uhoon-Soru' but also took its recipe, along with rice, and further developed it.

So, the Uhoon-Soru that made its way to the Arab nations, primarily Persia (modern-day Iran), returned as Biryani with the Mughals in the northern part of the subcontinent. It also reached the southern Tamil region, introduced by invading Muslim rulers and Arab traders, but gained prominence after the formation of British India. The name 'Biriyani' became a famous household name.

Today, however, Tamils still use Uhoon-Soru in different ways and names. Examples are ChickenRice (Kohli-Soru), PrawnRice (Era-Soru), and FishRice (Meen-Soru) to name a few. A vegan (or vegetarian) version of that is 'kulai-Soru' (Rice cooked with vegetables and spices). In Jaffna, 'Kohli-Pongal' (Red raw rice cooked with Chiken) is a special delicacy.

You can find more details later when we get into the recipe section.

CHAPTER 4

Introducing Curry to the British (Empire) India

The British East India Company started its trading activities at the beginning of the 17th century but the English civil war slowed its progress. They had trading posts in Madras (Chennai— The present-day capital of Tamils' state in India).

At that time, as we have seen, the Portuguese and Dutch had a strong presence in that region. However, the dowry of the Bombay area, which was part of Goa, by the Portuguese, to the English King Charles II, who came to the throne, just after the English civil war, gave the English a strong foothold.

It was a clever move by the English, as (in his own

admission), contrary to the expectation of Charles II, the princess who arrived in England was not attractive.

It was therefore a marriage for diplomatic purposes, and on the other hand, because of the dowry arrangement, the Portuguese were able to hold on to Goa, which was the longest colony in the continent (450 years between 1510 and 1961), even though the British became very powerful in India and the Portuguese became weak, and the Dutch had to cede control of all of their territories (Ceylon, Indonesia, Malacca, South Africa) to the British.

The Portuguese were the first and the last colonial power on the subcontinent as the British left India in 1947 and the French left Puducherry in 1954.

Robert Clive and the battle of Plassey

In 1757, the British East India Company sent Robert Clive, widely regarded as having laid the foundation stone for "British India", from Madras (Chennai) with reinforcements to re-establish the company's factories (trading stations) in Bengal that had been attacked and destroyed by the local Muslim ruler, who had received assistance from the French.

With 800 European soldiers and 3,000 local soldiers, Clive departed from Madras, a Tamil region (the present-day capital of Tamil Nadu state in India), to swiftly respond to the East India Company's request, ensuring the continuity of the company's business activities.

It wouldn't be an exaggeration to say that they were all curry enthusiasts, and through them, curry culture expanded to Bengal. Calcutta (Kolkata), the capital city of Bengal, eventually became the East India Company's headquarters and the first capital of 'British India'.

The East India Company became unstoppable after

defeating the French and, more crucially, the local ruler, Nawab Sirajuddaula of Bengal area. This offered it a rare opportunity to govern the region as well.

Please take note of the "beef link" between Europeans and the Tamils that is discussed below and note that what was gone along with Robert Clive and his Madras soldiers was undoubtedly non-vegetarian Muslim food based on beef that was subsequently introduced to the UK. (See the list of curry classifications below)

Even now, few restaurants offering non-vegetarian food in Tamil Nadu are referred to by the colonial phrase "Military cafe" (cafeteria - eatery).

Curry followed the British as they expanded its wings from Calcutta eastward, westward, and southward to conquer regions. In this way, the pre-chilli era curry of the Tamils was introduced into British India as well as modern Bangladesh, Burma, and Pakistan.

Yes, the claims of some British authors that the 'British introduced curry into India', was technically correct but misleading. Such authors fail to note that the British wouldn't have introduced something that was neither in the UK nor in any of its other colonies at that time apart from the Tamil area of Madras (Chennai) from where they departed.

Nonetheless, it's plausible that the British might have introduced new fruits, vegetables, and the Post-Chilli era Curry Powder, initially referred to as 'Madras Curry Powder,' from the Ceylon Tamils to the Indian Tamils, and subsequently to the rest of India after the establishment of British Ceylon.

Curry in British India

> **To make a Currey the Indian Way.**
> TAKE two small Chickens, skin them and cut them as for a Fricasey, wash them clean, and stew them in about a Quart of Water, for about five Minutes, then strain off the Liquor and put the Chickens in a clean Dish; take three large Onions, chop them small and fry them in about two Ounces of Butter, then put in the Chickens and fry them together till they are brown, take a quarter of an Ounce of Turmerick, a large Spoonful of Ginger and beaten Pepper together, and a little Salt to your Palate; strew all these Ingredients over the Chickens whilst it is frying, then pour in the Liquor, and let it stew about half an Hour, then put in a quarter of a Pint of Cream, and the Juice of two Lemons, and serve it up. The Ginger, Pepper, and Turmerick must be beat very fine.

Here's a famous curry recipe credited to one Hannah Glasse in 1747. The East India company was operating in Madras (Chennai) and Robert Clive just began as a writer there in 1744.

Hannah's recipe was clearly from a pre-chilli era (Black Pepper) from the Tamils of the Indian subcontinent. Recipes like this have led some authors to say that curry was introduced to India by the British. (I used to question whose curry they were referring to because surely curry couldn't have originated in the UK!). This recipe must have come to Britain when East India company began its trading activities in the 17th century.

However, the assertion that the ancient Tamil word curry was invented by English settlers who arrived in Madras (Chennai) in the 17th century, is just wrong...

On the other hand, it's important to note that the Tamils in Ceylon began substituting chilli for pepper in the Portuguese era began in the early 16th century.

The first curry house in London, Hindustani Coffee House, was opened in 1810 by a Bengali, Sake Dean Mahomed, a captain in the British East India Company and so many restaurants, nearly 90%, as of now owned by Bengali-speaking Bangladeshis. Another question that arises here is "what is the link between curry and Bangladesh"?

Well, Sake Dean Mahomed was never a chef but a trainee surgeon in the army of the East India Company. He had a good relationship with his superior officer who was from Ireland and with him, he moved to Cork in 1784, then at the turn of the new century, moved to London with his Irish wife and opened a restaurant in 1810, 26 years later after his arrival in the UK. A year later, it was shut down due to poor business.

Important fact to note: Pre-chilli era curry

Sake Dean Mahomed arrived in the UK in 1784, at a

time when the two areas of the Island of Ceylon were still Dutch colonies. It wasn't until 1796 that these two areas of Ceylon came under British rule. Therefore, the curry introduced into the UK, as well as into British India, Bangladesh, Pakistan, and Burma, was predominantly of Tamil origin from British India. It was not the curry of the island's Tamils, where curry underwent a renaissance for 300 years under the Portuguese and Dutch.

We may now agree that the 'Indian' Curry Recipe of Hannah Glasse in 1747 is showing us clearly that, since it is mentioning only black pepper and not chilli (that Portuguese brought to the Tamils 249 years earlier in 1498) and so it was the pre-chilli era.

This point is important in solving the confusions about curry today.

Remember what we discussed earlier, the Tamils' introduction to new vegetables by the Europeans led to the curry renaissance, which was not just fuelled by chilli and chilli powder. The main reason why Tamils in the southern Indian subcontinent didn't quickly embrace the post-chilli development of curry was their suspicion of the Europeans due to their aggressive colonial policies, which included the spread of Christianity in other regions. Furthermore, contacts between the two Tamil regions were largely severed, at least until both regions came under British rule. Following the Slavery Abolition Act of 1833, the British authorities in India transported a large number of Indian Tamils to other British territories.

Thus, we now have South African Curry, Caribbean Curry, Burmese Curry, Vietnamese Curry, South African Curry, Mauritian Curry, Singaporean Curry, and Malaysian curry. Except for the last two, all were pre-chilli era curry and not related to the curry renaissance that took place under the Portuguese and Dutch.

The British also took migrants from India to Malacca but because it was a Portuguese and Dutch colony before their arrival and also because the British offered civil service postings to educated Ceylon Tamils (see below), Malaysia and Singapore today have a mix of pre- and post-chilli era curries.

Partition and Pakistan

Following independence in 1947, Bengal split into West Bengal, part of India and East Bengal became East Pakistan. In the 1970s East Pakistan became Bangladesh but its civil war sent thousands away as refugees and may eventually arrived in Britain too.

Once here, some followed the restaurant business. The Hindustani Coffee House and as noted earlier, a very high percentage of 'Indian' Curry Houses in the UK, are today owned and run by Bangladeshis.

Another point worth mentioning here is the relationship between Europeans and the Tamils of the Islamic faith (Tamil Muslims) when it comes to non-vegetarian food, especially beef. The majority of the Tamils and or others are mostly Hindus, Jains, and Buddhists who for religious reasons do not eat beef while, and for the same reason, Muslims do not consume pork. Whereas most Europeans consume both.

As a result, there was a natural beef-consuming relationship between Europeans and Tamil Muslims. And serving beef to British forces in India was more cost-effective than feeding them with mutton, chicken, or seafood, so Muslim chefs among the Tamils were early on recruited by the East India Company in Madras.

These chefs must have travelled with Robert Clive and

his forces to the battlefield of Plassey and later into Bengal, the main city of which was Calcutta which was the very first capital of British India. In their relentless mission of empire expansion, the British forces were accompanied by Curry and the trustworthy chefs as they marched throughout the subcontinent.

Indeed, a Muslim chef, 'Abdul Karim (the Munshi)' became a favourite chef of Queen Victoria, who was said to be a great curry fan. However, the chef Munshi was from Northern India and so even the greatest empress that the world has ever seen would not have tasted the authentic curry.

It is important to remember that she was reigning over the two regions where the Tamil people traditionally live.

Queen Victoria with 'Munshi'

Chapter 5

Pinning down the definition of Curry

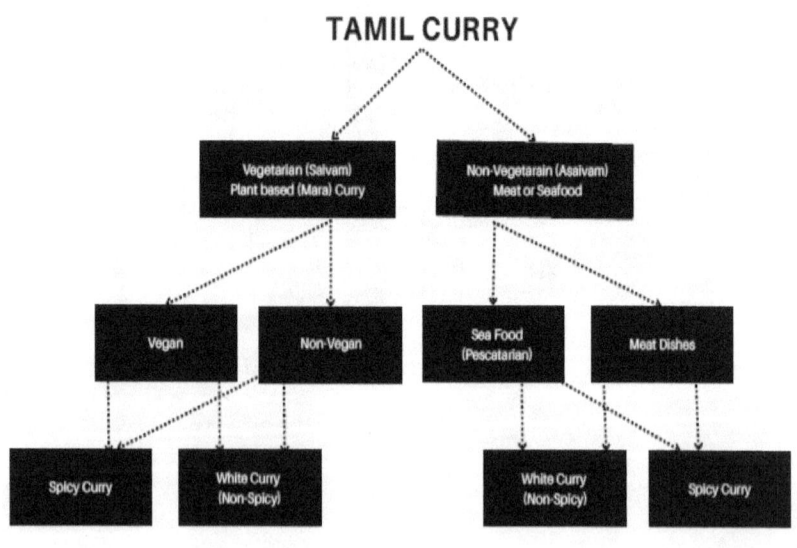

Among the Tamils, 'Saiva Meal' and 'Asaiva Meal' are colloquial terms for vegetarian and non-vegetarian meals, respectively. 'Saiva' is a sub-sect of Hinduism. But among the Tamils, Saivam (சைவம்) and Asaivam (அசைவம்) refer to veg and non-veg food, respectively. Though the first word also refers to Tamils who worship Lord Shiva, a Hindu god, and remember, they don't normally eat beef.

I have spent some time discussing all this with Tamil scholars in a bid to figure out when and how the usage of these words came about. I now think that these essentially religious distinctions emerged after the Arab Muslims started trading with the Tamils for their spices and some Tamils adopted Islam. Eid al-Adha, or the "Feast of Sacrifice' and the distribution by affluent traders of fresh meat, cooked meat, or meat curry, (mainly beef) and biryani to the poor might be part of the reason that today we have these terms and distinctions.

For example, today in Tamil areas, the making and sharing of 'fasting Congee' (Nonbu Congee) during Ramadan by Tamils of the Islamic faith is widespread. Congees – typically a rice-based porridge – are delicious and the Nonpu Congee is super delicious as we will see the recipe later.

As Christianity grew (which did not restrict the consumption of any meat, including pork and beef), usage of these phrases must have increased after the Portuguese brought chilli to the Tamil people, shortly after the Middle Ages.

Personally, though, I do like to eat beef sometimes. When I was at high school, back home, 'roti and roast beef curry' in the neighbourhood 'Bhai-kade' was always my first choice – as it was for my friends. It has a unique kind of taste, indeed.

Curry heritage of the Tamils

So as you can see, the non-vegetarian, Muslim meals along with Mohul Islamic rulers' Samosa and Biriyani dishes have come to the UK and so they have no answers to the demand for vegan or vegetarian curries. At the same time, we find opportunistic attempts to re-invent vegan curries for the new markets.

Today, you can even find the Prime Minister of Canada playfully preparing the Tamils' wildly popular 'Koththu Roti' (Koththu Paratha) at a Tamil food festival. This dish can be made with some vegetables and aslo with any meat such as chicken, beef, mutton, or seafood. 'Koththu' means 'chopping,' and the 'Roti' and other ingredients are chopped together using a special tool on a griddle. If you've never experienced the delight of 'Koththu Roti', I recommend it as you're in for a real Tamil culinary treat.

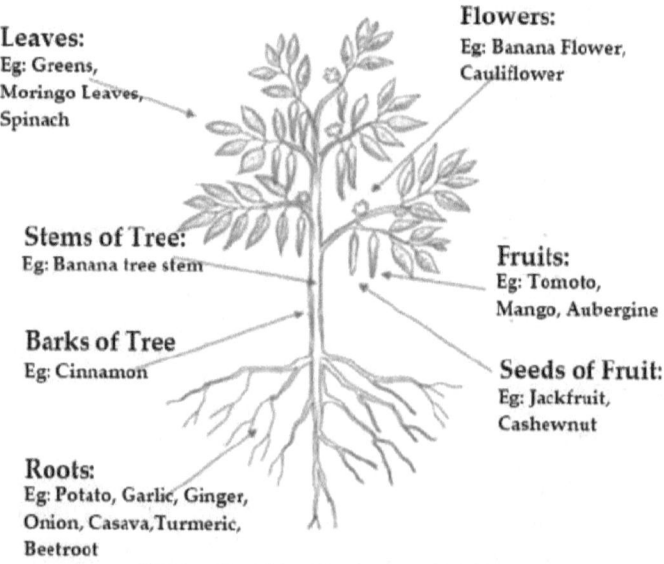

Mara(k) Curry or Plant based Curry

Leaves:
Eg: Greens, Moringo Leaves, Spinach

Flowers:
Eg: Banana Flower, Cauliflower

Stems of Tree:
Eg: Banana tree stem

Fruits:
Eg: Tomoto, Mango, Aubergine

Barks of Tree
Eg: Cinnamon

Seeds of Fruit:
Eg: Jackfruit, Cashewnut

Roots:
Eg: Potato, Garlic, Ginger, Onion, Casava, Turmeric, Beetroot

'Maram' in Tamil means plant or tree

Tamil people who consume vegetarian meals refer to it as a 'Saiva meal' or as 'Mara(k) Curry meals', both of which have the same meaning. (The word 'maram' in Tamil refers to plants – 'plant based' food).

The name 'Kaai-Curry meal' is also used by some Tamils. Kaai is the Tamil word for unripe fruit, and 'pazham' is the word for mature fruit. As we've already seen, the word 'Kaai-Curry' refers to dishes made with unripe fruit or berries. Unripe sour Mango curry is an example of Kaai Curry.

The same goes for unripe jackfruit curry too. On the other hand, a non-vegetarian (seafood or meat) dish is called a 'Machcha Curry'.

The Dutch introduced the breadfruit and a curry on it is very popular among the Tamils in the island, while it is not popular in India except in few areas of Chera land of Kerala.

British India and British Ceylon

After the British victory at the Battle of Plassey in 1757 against both the French and the local rulers followed by the seizure of Calcutta and Bengal, Britain's colonial ambitions in the Indian subcontinent really began to take off. Although the coastal regions (Coromandel) already had several European trading ports, now the British became the first to colonise the Tamil regions in the south of the Indian subcontinent, which had previously been free of any European influence. In 1796, after nearly finishing the conquest of the entire Indian subcontinent, they arrived in Ceylon and gained control from the Dutch. A new unified nation, British Ceylon' was formed in 1833 after the British had fully established their authority.

Almost all of the Indian subcontinent was captured and, as mentioned earlier, the East India Company Limited was running an empire on its own with two countries firmly under its thumb. However, it should be noted again that some three hundred years prior to the start of the British era, the Portuguese and Dutch had assisted the Tamils in Ceylon to experience a curry renaissance.

As explained earlier, British Ceylon was a crown colony from 1798 onwards and in 1858, the British Parliament dissolved the East India company, and the British India came under the direct rule of the British government. However, it should be noted that the British decided to administer India and Ceylon separately.

Once the boat services between Tamils were established on both sides of Palk Strait (The strait is named after Robert Palk, who was a governor of Madras from 1755–1763).

It was while under the British that the new food recipes of the Portuguese and Dutch era, with their newly introduced vegetables as well as chilli and curry powder, started spreading amongst across to the Tamil communities of Southern India.

Numerous novelties from north India, such as Sappati, Poori, Samosas, Naan and seekh kebab also made their way to the southwards at the same time.

One such dish that gained enormous popularity during the British era and spread both down south to the island of Ceylon was the dish we know as biryani. However, the spread of new recipes between the Tamil areas was slow and that may be due to affordability and the fear of the unknown. Nonetheless, recent economic advancements and social media growth are expediting this now.

On the other hand, cooking with chilli propagated rapidly throughout India during the British era. This was due to the fact that relative calm was achieved under British administration, as the subcontinent was constantly at war with its numerous kingdoms, sultanates, queendoms, and chiefdoms. (The same relative calm imposed by the Portuguese and Dutch over nearly three hundred years earlier, had contributed to the island's curry renaissance.)

The Tamils on the sub-continent may have been exposed to the outcome of the island Tamils' curry renaissance (and the new vegetables that helped it), by the British when both countries were firmly under the British rule.

Madras Curry Powder: Mild, Hot and Very Hot

It was while British India was still under colonial rule that a new variety of curry powder, called Madras Curry Powder, started to appear on the market.

To start with, the introduction of this product was not very successful, perhaps because the product fell short of the standard set by the islet's first-ever curry powder. This family recipe, known as 'Curry Thuool' (both are Tamil words meaning curry powder), had been constantly enhanced for more than three hundred years and now three hundred years.

Even though Madras (now Chennai) is the capital city of the Tamil Nadu state of India, and Madras Curry Powder is not a widely known brand in Tamil Nadu or in India but can be seen in the shelves of major supermarkets in the west, it can't compete with the 'Curry Paste' despite its short shelf life. Curry Paste was not a novel innovation, as the producers claimed, but rather a pre-chilli era mix of the Tamils, that had been heavily altered without any knowledge of its origins.

And both (Madras Curry Powder and the Curry Paste) come to the market as Mild, Hot and Very Hot which clearly indicate that the manufactures have no idea of them at all!

It is important to understand, that 'curry paste' or 'Curry Thuool' (Curry Powder) must always be made with the ingredients in correct ratio: The manufactures should not change this ratio for it to be mild, hot and very hot. It should be the users who must decide how many spoons to be added to the dish so that it can be mild, hot or very hot. It's like adding sugar to tea or coffee. How many spoons? It is the users' choice, right?

Anyway, Madras Curry Powder became known for not having 'roasted ingredients' in the correct ratio whereas the Portuguese–Tamil collaborative preparation involves carefully roasting the ingredients individually at a suitable temperature for each to achieve the perfect quality. Only a few families have that secret recipe which is passed down between generations.

Curry spreads all round the world

In terms of recipe, when compared to the Portuguese and Dutch, the British contribution to the curry renaissance is much less. However, the British helped to spread curry to other parts of the world particularly by taking Tamil chefs and other Tamil workers to other parts of British India and the other colonies.

Thus, curry spread to Northern, Eastern, and Western India including present-day Pakistan, Bangladesh, and Burma (Myanmar) which were parts of British India.

By taking the Tamils as immigrant workers to Burma, Mauritius, Malaysia, Fiji, South Africa, Reunion Islands, Seychelles, and the Caribbean (Guyana, Trinidad, Tobago, Suriname, Guadeloupe and Martinique) the taste for curry spread there too.

Likewise, most of the Tamil people who live in Mauritius are from the southern state of Tamil Nadu and have been there since 1727 to work on the sugar cane plantations. And there is an island in the Indian Ocean called Reunion that is still owned by France.

As indentured labors, primarily from Pondicherry and Karaikal, the French colonies in Southern India, Tamil settlements began as early as 1848. (Note that the former prime minister of Guyana, "Moses Nagamootoo," is of a Tamil descent.)

And because both the two traditional habitats of the Tamils came under the British, so there were two types of Tamils during the British colonial era. One was in India as 'Indian Tamils' and one was on the island of Ceylon as 'Ceylon Tamils' (now known as Sri Lankan Tamils).

The Indian Tamils have something of a food dilemma as India is their country now and so when it comes to 'Indian Curry', they understandably became patriotic without any idea of the curry crisis in the UK. Hence, it falls to me as a Tamil living in the UK and also as a person who was born and brought up in the islet village that was the very first exclusive Portuguese Tamil colony, to come out and clarify the curry issue.

First though, it is interesting to look further into these two Tamil groups in order to understand curry more from their different points of view.

There were (and still are) successful merchants or traders among the Indian Tamils popularly known as 'Chettiars' who were the counterpart of European Jews and dominated the finance sector in all British Empire in the Far East and Africa. These Chettiars were in business since the first millennia and the post-Sangam period Tamils literature **Silapathikaraaram** and **Manimeghalai** also has references to that.

They were rich and had a good relationship with the British administrators of all colonies where they did business. Some owned ships to move merchandise as they travelled around well between other British colonies to do trade, and since they were affluent, they were able to have luxury food and so 'Chettinad' curry recipes evolved among them. Chetty Nadu (short: 'Chettinad') refers to the area or countryside in Tamil Nadu state where Chettyars hail.

These recipes are both vegetarian and non-vegetarian (except of course, the meat did not include beef). We will see that too and note that these are post-chilli eras (because of their overseas connection to Ceylon, Malaysia and Thailand.)

Grand palaces, which are still in use and are incredibly 'luxurious' by Indian standards, serve as evidence of the Chettiars' affluence. Waddesdon Manor, a Jewish family-owned mansion in England at the time can be compared to theirs. The lack of gardens in these mansions suggests that Chetty Nadu hadn't adopted Englishman Lancelot "Capability" Brown's idea of gardening.

It was after defeating Nawab Sirajuddaula, who had been backed by the French, at the Battle of the Plassey in 1757, that Robert Clive and the East India Company's men took control of the Bengal region. And when Calcutta was chosen as the (first) Capital of British India in 1774, they required "honest and trustworthy middlemen" to negotiate with the natives and construct their first-ever governmental framework.

The Chettiars, a subgroup of the Tamil community who originated from Chettinad in Tamil Nadu and traditionally, were involved in the trade of precious stones were chosen by the British because they believed they were the most qualified for the position. They earned their trust and were later on the first to open shops in all the main towns throughout the British colonies, including Calcutta's 'Ezra Street'.

Beginning in the 1850s, wealthy Chettiars came to Burma, and by the 1930s, they had established all over the country. By 1941, the Chettiar families had 300,000 acres of arable land in addition to 700 stores in Malaya, 450 in Ceylon, and 105 in Indonesia. In Burma alone, they ran 1,655 shops.

As mentioned just, the Chettiars had a long history in the trading of precious stones, but they later transitioned into private banking and money lending, establishing themselves in Singapore as early as the 1820s.

They went into business in Vietnam, a French territory, as well as in Malaysia, Burma, Singapore, Mauritius, Reunion, South Africa, Ceylon, and Thailand. And everywhere they went, Curry accompanied them too.

Following their victory at the Battle of Plassey, the East India Company gained confidence and started building an empire on its own. In their wake came American missionaries who came to Calcutta to spread Christianity. However, after the Anglo–American war of 1812, the suspicious East India Company's management in Calcutta ordered the American Missionary members to leave and, on their way out, they passed in transit through Jaffna in Northern Ceylon.

Some of them then made the decision to stay, and by 1818 they had started missionary schools on the Jaffna peninsula. Students attending these missionary institutions were prepared for the London Matriculation Exams. This is partly why the educated 'Ceylon Tamils' were offered civil service jobs by the British Administration in Southern India, Singapore, Malaysia, Burma, Fiji, South Africa, and Mauritius. They were the link between the British administration and the illiterate Tamils and other migrants from India.

From my village, many moved too and my maternal grandfather was recruited as a civil service officer for Malaysia, my mother and three more, out of five of her siblings, were born there before eventually returning to Ceylon after World War II.

These affluent groups of people too travelled well and their quality of life improved and so they too developed new

Curry heritage of the Tamils

non-vegetarian and vegetarian curry recipes. For this, curry powder helped immensely.

And then there was also another group, known as the 'Brahmins': the Hindu priests and their families. These had different vegetarian curry recipes and adhere to a strict vegetarian diet.

They didn't eat eggs but instead saw eggs as a non-vegetarian food, but they did consume dairy products like Ghee (cow butter), Curd (yoghurt), and Milk, and so therefore they are not vegans. (We have already seen the 'Saiva' vegetarian classification and the Brahmin can be non-vegan and the rest can be vegan.).

Contrary to Brahmins, another tribe is well-known for its non-vegetarian curry cuisine. These are the Tamils of the Islamic faith. (Tamil Muslims). Except for pork, they are particularly well-liked for non-vegan food. Even today, 'Bhai Kades' (cafes) are common and frequently the first choice in Tamils when it comes to meat-based non-vegetarian food. (Note that the Tamil word for shop or outlet is kade or kadai.) These Tamil Muslims were the originators of one of the most well-known dishes, 'Koththu Roti' (Koththu in Tamil means chopped, and another word for Roti is 'Paratha').

Most people in the West and the UK have yet to experience this delicious dish at their dinner tables. The layered soft wheat roti of the Tamils – 'Koththu' is made with this

As mentioned above, recently, in a Tamil street festival, Justin Trudeau, the Canadian Prime Minister could be found making Koththu Roti (Koththu Parota) for fun. A special tool is used to chop the Roti (Paratha) and the meat curry and vegetables while being cooked in a girdle. The dish is a very popular Tamil delicacy of the post-chilli era but has yet to reach the dinner tables in the west.

How come, then, did the Canadian Prime Minister know about the dish? Well, numerous Tamils were sent abroad as refugees and migrants during the protracted civil conflict in Sri Lanka. And, as of right now, Canada is home to the majority of Sri Lankan Tamils living outside of their native north and east of Sri Lanka.

The UK has the second-largest number of Tamils followed by Australia, France, Germany, Scandinavia, and Switzerland. The Tamils are becoming very strong in politics with an MP in the Canadian parliament and in the Cabinet and many as councillors in London boroughs and Canadian local bodies. There are a few in Australia, Norway, France, and Switzerland too. And all of them brought the post-chilli era curry with them. And in September 2023, a Ceylon (Sri Lankan) Tamil descendant became the President of Singapore.

All the groups mentioned use innovative but authentic curry recipes and we will see many of their recipes soon. They have developed many vegetable curries and food items which are delicious and unfamiliar in the West.

There are area-specific recipes too (like Welsh Cake or Yorkshire Pudding) which will appear here in the recipe section. For example, in Ceylon, vinegar and grinded mustard added to curries or pickles (fish pickles, prawn pickles, and beef pickles) are popular and these were developed during Dutch colonial times.

In Tamil Nadu, Kumbakonam Kadappa, Madurai bun paratha (Dough for Roti-Paratha rolled like bun and shallow fried), Chithamparam Aubergine Kotsu, and Thirunelveli Maapilai Sothy (a curry to honour the bride-groom) are to name but a few. Not to forget some secret, colonial-era curry recipes too, like 'Thurai Curry'.

'Thurai' in Tamil means someone powerful or with authority, usually referring to British colonial era local administrators, such as district administrators or collectors of Taxes or even Judges. Their favourite recipe/s was known then as ,'Thurai's curry' in Tamil Nadu. (English word closely matching 'Thurai', could be, 'Lord'). In British Ceylon, devilled beef, devilled chicken, devilled prawns, etc. are examples of this.

If we look into the history of Malaysia (and Singapore) then we can see a clear link. First, it was a Portuguese colony (1511-1641) and it was Dutch (1641-1824) followed by the British (1824-1948). Same pattern as that of Ceylon Tamils.

Further, all five groups mentioned above migrated to Malaysia during the British period. As discussed elsewhere in this book, the Tamil Muslim's non-veg tradition was preferred by the Europeans, especially because of the beef link, and the British introduced these in Bengal and the rest of India, and then it came to the UK.

But both Indian and Ceylon Tamils who migrated to other colonies were mostly Hindus and so what they have taken with them was not non-veg Muslim curries. However, there were Tamil Muslim migrants too and so Biryani and beef dishes travelled too.

The Europeanised Tamil Curry

As I have been saying, whenever anyone talks about 'Indian Curry', they confuse the issue of authenticity. If we look at a mulligatawny recipe published on 12 Jan 2017 in The Guardian newspaper by Felicity Cloake it illustrates this confusion. Here is an extract from that recipe article.

According to Lizzie Collingham's excellent Curry: A Tale of Cooks and Conquerors, "mulligatawny soup was one of the earliest dishes to emerge from the new hybrid cuisine which the British developed in India, combining British concepts of how food should be presented ... and Indian recipes".

Madhur Jaffrey describes it as "a classic of the mixed-race, Anglo-Indian community in India" and "an essential part of my childhood", while Colonel Arthur Robert Kenney-Herbert, author of the 1878 recipe collection, Culinary Jottings for Madras, recommends it as a "really excellent, and at times, most invigorating soup". Mulligatawny doesn't deserve to be hidden away at the top of the menu, outshone by samosas and seekh kebabs. Made with care, this unapologetically old-fashioned, gently spiced fusion classic is, as Jaffrey puts it, "really a curry, a meal in itself".

To read more, scan the QR code below with your camera:

But are these notes correct? It wouldn't have been necessary to use the colloquial (informal) Tamil term 'Mulligatawny' in place of the English term 'Black Pepper Soup' if it had been developed by the British, who, after all, were then the ruling elite with authority.

No, both the curry and the Mulligatawny of the Tamils have been around for thousands of years. However, although other Europeans have used them before the British, it is the British who introduced them to a dinner table with style and manners to be talked about. (Further down, you will see a case study on Mulligatawny.) For example, the traditional culture of the Tamils was to eat by sitting on the floor and eating rice and curry off a banana leaf.

It was Portuguese who introduced table (Mesa in Portuguese) to the Tamils and the word 'Mesai' (with an 'i' at the end) is in Tamil language referring to previously unknown furniture; table! Many Portuguese words are in Tamil language and another popular one is 'janel', which means 'window'.

Compared to the Portuguese and Dutch of the 15th to 17th century who were largely illiterate, the British officials of the 19th and 20th century were highly educated with the governors and senior civil servants likely Oxbridge or similar university graduates. (For example, First governor of Ceylon Frederick North was an Oxford Graduate and Henry Monck-

Mason Moore, the last governor of Ceylon was a Cambridge graduate.)

Naturally, they introduced the concept of how food should be presented.

These educated British Officials elevated themselves above the top of the class or caste system, and as a result, their mannerisms and personal styles made English language education appealing throughout the British Empire and is still popular and shows no sign of disappearing which was unlike that of Portuguese or Dutch languages.

In conclusion, the British didn't bother to develop curry in either India or Ceylon, despite what Lizzie Collingham claims in her book. However, they made sure that the curry was brought to dining tables and presented in a way that would appeal to the wealthy, educated upper class.

On the other hand, curry really cannot be discussed without mentioning the significant contributions of the Dutch and Portuguese. Since at least five hundred years ago, the Portuguese had already revamped and Europeanised the curry of the island Tamils by working with them.

To me, it is disheartening that some authors restrict Portuguese influence to Goa, their sole colony in India. This is problematic for curry studies because Goa is a non-Tamil region.

The undeniable fact was, there was no post-chilli era curry of the Tamils, without the Portuguese and the chilli and other vegetables they brought in. The British came into the picture nearly three hundred years later after Portuguese and the Dutch.

Curry in Britain

Ever since non-natives (meaning non-Tamils) began to seriously introduce the curry, what has been happening in Britain is trying to re-invent Europeanisation while failing terribly! Take the recipe for Chicken Tikka Masala, which is commonly referred to as a British curry. This is uses double

Curry heritage of the Tamils

cream and is consequently an unhealthy, fatty curry.

It would be better for non-Tamils to take up what the Portuguese and Dutch left behind with the Tamils because it had already been Europeanised and also authentic.

In a moment, I will introduce recipes as a set that are from both habitats of the Tamils. Also, I will introduce some new curry-related Tamil words and ancient phrases like Kulampu, Warai, Sothi, Koththu-Roti, and super desserts like Watilappam, Paayasam, and Doddal to name a few.

But remember, the entire goal of this book is to regain the public's and government's support in order to save the curry industry from impending collapse, not to belittle non-Tamil initiatives on British territory.

And so, finally, here is an example of what is now taking on in the UK's curry sector. This is, in my opinion, just the tip of the iceberg.

Mulligatawny soup

Ainsley Harriot	Hainz
Ingredients Glucose syrup, potato starch, natural flavourings (**WHEAT**), sugar, salt, vegetables (1.7% tomato powder, 0.9% carrot, celeriac powder (**CELERY**)), palm oil, 2.3% curry spices (paprika, cumin, fenugreek, cardamom, cinnamon, chilli, clove, turmeric, pimento), herbs (coriander, parsley), rapeseed oil, **BARLEY** malt extract, **MILK** protein, flavourings, emulsifier (E471). Allergy Advice For allergies, including cereals containing gluten, see ingredients in **BOLD**. Storage Store in a cool, dry place. Best Before End See bottom of pack. Made with responsibly sourced palm oil.	**ingredients** Water, Tomatoes (38%), Apples, Beef (6%), Rice (2%), Sugar, Modified Cornflour, Rapeseed Oil, Curry Powder (contains Wheat Flour, Celery, Mustard), Wheat Flour (contains Calcium, Iron, Niacin, Thiamin), Salt, Flavourings, Colour - Plain Caramel

This simple example explains the issue of curry. We have already seen that 'Mulligatawny' is another Tamil word that came into the English Language and the original wording is Millaku-Tawny). These are two Tamil words together; Black Pepper (Millaku) and Water (Tawny)), which means Black Pepper Tonic or Soup

.Yet often, the Black Pepper is missing from the ingredients!

This is like an APPLE PIE without any APPLES in it!

One is sold in cans and is from a $25 billion corporation Haynes, that instead includes beef and apple (which is not native fruit in the Tamil areas and so can't be expected), while the other is sold in sachet from a celebrity chef, Harriott who appears on TV, and doesn't use beef.

See another example: Walkers, a well-known brand in the market for crisps who is selling Poppadom in packets. Guess what; no black gram (urid dhal) in the ingredient list. Poppadom is a Tamil word and there is no Poppadom without black gram.

Let me also mention another Tamil word 'Rasam'. This is the basic version of 'Mulligatawny' (sic) or correctly Milaku-Tawny. Rasam, a herb based soup, is consumed just before, with, or after a curry meals. Rasam is commonly added to food to improve digestion and relieve gas problems in the stomach. The soup is made by dissolving tamarind in water, adding salt and spice powders, and boiling ; it is called 'Puli Rasam' (Puli in Tamil means Sour). It is very popular among the Tamils. Generally, rice and curry lunch is served with Rasam.

Curry heritage of the Tamils

The curry paste in bottles available in supermarkets is also very different from what the Tamils make. The use of traditional Tamil "curry paste" goes all the way back to before the introduction of the chilli (pre-chilli era). Pre-Chilli era Curry paste, which is still being used occasionally with its ancient characteristics (no chillies), was mainly replaced with curry powder in the post-chilli era.

Individuals often develop their own concepts and label them as innovative, especially when unchallenged by the actual owners of curry, the Tamils. This situation has led to confusion within the market, as is evident today. However, when the market seeks clarification on matters of authenticity, there is often a lack of responsible responses, leaving everyone frustrated.

A Tamil proverb wisely conveys the message: "He who carries a stick thinks of himself as a hunter," but its true meaning is quite the opposite. It suggests that just having the tools does not make one an expert; experience and knowledge are essential. Similarly, in my humble opinion, those who commercialise curry without understanding its rich history act as opportunistic entities. Their actions often lead to market confusion, contributing to the ongoing curry crisis. Authenticity issues like these are a significant challenge that corporations grapple with in this field today.

As a result, curry enthusiasts are unable to taste the authentic variety and frequently become frustrated, giving up on curry altogether.

CHAPTER 6

Responding to the Curry Crisis

Talks in the curry industry are about the Great British curry crisis. But what exactly is it?

Some say that the crisis stems from the fact that the curry industry never emerged from being a family-type business into becoming a more corporate business. Some say it is rooted in the UK government's policy of not issuing enough visas to chefs. And others, more broadly, point at a lack of innovation.

In the article I mentioned earlier, titled 'The Great British Curry Crisis'. Malcolm Moore analysed many issues that the curry industry faces including that:

"The British public is coming to an awareness that what these curry houses are serving is not real Indian food."

But then the obvious question arises: if the food being served in 'Curry Houses' is not real, then what is authentic curry and where is it? In the market, there are hundreds of cookbooks with fancy names like 'Curry', 'Secret of Curry', 'The Indian Curry', 'The Best Indian Curry' recipes, and so on.

These cookbooks have been written by natives of both Indian and Westerners. However, they are all using the same phrase, "Curry of India", a term which unifies them all. But when journalists or scholars visit Indian cities they are invariably surprised to find that not a single curry popular in UK restaurants is known in India let alone offered in Indian eateries.

Robin Cook and the British Curry

There is an intriguing story about the former British Foreign Secretary, Robin Cook, during his state visit to India. He expressed a desire to enjoy his favorite curry but was surprised to find that none of Delhi's renowned chefs were familiar with the recipe. Upon his return, the Foreign Secretary famously declared that Chicken Tikka Masala is genuinely a British creation. It was almost as if Britain was adopting an orphaned dish, unable to find its rightful owners!

What's particularly revealing about a statement like that, made by a representative of such a powerful institution as the government, is that it highlights the uncertainty surrounding the authenticity of curry within the British government itself.

It's worth noting that Malcom Moore, the journalist mentioned earlier, also employs the term "Indian food.

Curry heritage of the Tamils

We discussed the merit of this earlier when we noted that curry has been around for more than 3000 years, long before India was formed as a nation by the British colonial administration.

In fact, the British Curry industry is largely dominated by immigrants from Bangladesh while the other important ingredient of curry in the West, the curry paste market, and various curry-related sources and pickles are dominated by immigrants from Eastern Africa.

These neglected geographical facts are partly why today curry houses cannot convince the British Government that the food they serve is authentically Indian, or authentically Bangladeshi, as the Government knows well that no one can point out that a curry that is being served in Britain is coming out of a region in India or Bangladesh. As a result, the UK government shied away from issuing more chef visas but instead set up a Parliamentary Curry Group in 2015 to consider the issues facing the curry industry.

In fact, the government of David Cameron asked the curry industry that wanted the government to provide more visas to foreign chefs, to instead train locals to become chefs, and even invested £1.5 million for a training facility. However the project stalled due to a lack of interest.

At the same time, for example, a large number of applicants from the Sylhet region of Bangladesh requested chef visas, but an inquiry by the authorities revealed that they do not prepare or consume same food (Indian or British Curry in Bangladesh) in which they claimed to be expert chefs.

To make this point understandable, visas were requested so that Bangladeshi chefs could travel to the UK and prepare a special dish of (British) Curry that was not available in either Bangladesh or India and so they need training once in the UK. I think that the government's stance was understandable. After all, it seemed that the chefs needed to be trained or retrained here because those requesting the visas could not demonstrate that they are preparing or eating the same food at home.

The government must have considered along the lines of, "Why not allow locals who may be unemployed and receiving government assistance to receive training to become chefs instead." – This influenced the decision of establishing the £1.5million training facility.

However, as Malcom Moore of the Financial Times argued, the curry crisis is not really one of chefs and visas, but rather, more fundamentally, one of authenticity, or perhaps I should say, to be more precise, of originality.

No one can blame the public and the government for trying to establish authenticity when curries are available in so many different versions and forms and the chefs' visas are requested by people from different nations: Indian Curry, Bangladeshi Curry, Pakistan Balti Curry, Sri Lankan Curry, Malaysian Curry, Indonesian Curry, Korean Curry, Chinese Curry, Japanese Curry, Thai Red and Green Curry, Caribbean Curry – and lately Vietnamese Curry – to name a few, are in the market and no one can say with evidence that their one is truly authentic.

And yet this authenticity issue is preventing the curry industry from emerging into a corporate business like that of pizza or pasta, linked to Italy, Hamburgers linked to America, Noodles linked to China,

Peri - Peri source in Nando's linked to Portugal, or Tacos linked to Mexico.

Because no one can say with certainty that 'this is the standard curry' as so many people have their own ideas – like the one we have seen above concerning Mulligatawny soup.

Curry heritage of the Tamils

The end result is that British Curry houses are limiting themselves to being small pockets of family businesses. Those that had corporate aspirations have ultimately failed.

Authenticity issues and related confusion mean that curry houses serve biryani and samosas which are Arab dishes, Naan or Chapati or thalli (rice-centred) which are north Indian dishes and not related to traditional Tamil curry foods.

Consider the case of a Frenchman teaching French in China – he's likely to be successful. However, if he attempts to teach Russian there simply because of high demand, even if he's competent, he'll face challenges, as many individuals from various nations except Russians try to do the same. It all comes down to authenticity.

Curry made the corporate way –successes and failures.

Many people are puzzled as to why corporate businesses have had unsuccessful efforts to promote curry, considering it's a market worth £4.5 billion and a national favorite.

It all comes back to authenticity once more. As we have seen with the Mulligatawny soup (black pepper soup), when authenticity is lacking, there won't be uniformity in what is offered to customers because everyone will have different tastes or ideas.

Unlike McDonald's, Pizza Hut, or KFC, where you can expect the same taste worldwide due to their standardized offerings, regional variations in curry, such as Glasgow's versus Birmingham's, contribute to the challenge in promoting it as a uniform corporate product. Customers prefer consistency, as it ensures they know exactly what to expect each time they order.

This explains the remarkable success of the corporate company Nando's, which has approximately 470 outlets in the UK and Ireland alone, despite being around for just thirty years. A key factor contributing to its success is its signature curry sauce, 'peri-peri.' Yes, peri-peri is indeed a type of 'standardised' curry sauce and because of that customers know what they will be tasting and so returning.

Wagamama is a restaurant chain that opened the same year as Nando's and serves 7 million **Japanese "katsu chicken curries"** annually. Customers are aware that the overall taste of the 'peri-peri' sauce and the katsu curry will remain the same always. But this is NOT the case with 'Indian' curry served across the country. This can only be expected when Indian curry houses operate as pockets of 'family businesses'.

According to the UK media, young people are willing to stand in queues outside of these two restaurants during peak hours to get a seat. On the other hand, it should also be noted that, curry industry experts wonder why these youngsters are ditching Indian curry houses and, as we noted earlier, one key person suggested it is because of fatty curries that are being served.

In my opinion, the reason why these two multinational corporate businesses are successful is that they inadvertently introduced element of post-chilli era curry to the UK, which is tired of pre-chilli kind offered by the Indian curry houses.

To be clear to the reader: the Japanese Katsu Curry recipe includes, curry powder and coconut milk and therefore is definitely post-chilli era, the result of Portuguese - Tamil connection to Japan which we discussed earlier. Likewise, Singapore noodles, a speciality on the menus of Chinese restaurants and takeaways in the UK, are made with curry powder, indicating that they are a post-Chilli era delicacy.

It's possible that none of the parties mentioned above are aware of this fact as this is the first book to discuss about pre-chilli era curry, post-chilli era curry, curry renaissance and the Portuguese and Dutch links to the curry of the Tamils that existed before the British era.

Distinguishing between Indian Curry and Tamil Curry

The term "Indian Curry" has no real meaning and is not used anywhere in India, which is a union of several separate nations with diverse food cultures of the subcontinent. As we know, the phrase is mostly used in the West. This was the cause of Robin Cook's disappointment in Delhi mentioned above. At the very least, he would not have made that well-known assertion if he had conducted that search in the Tamil regions of South India or Sri Lanka.

India is a country formed by the British in its colonial era. Hundreds, if not thousands, of chiefdoms, Sultanates, Kingdoms, and Queendoms were conquered and the whole sub-continent amalgamated as one to form India.

In history, it was the British who redesigned the WHOLE Indian subcontinent into one entity. No wonder, when they left in 1947, Pakistan along with present-day Bangladesh immediately separated and Burma was already an independent country.

Actually, long before the British, there was an Emperor Ashoka (268–232 BC) of the Maurya Dynasty, who reigned over a combined subcontinent. During his reign, Buddhism spread throughout Southeast Asia including Thailand, China, Korea and Japan. Ashoka's empire stretched from Afghanistan to Bengal. But there's an important exception: he never ruled over the southern tip of Indian subcontinent where the Tamils lived.

However, let's go back to the question we started with: to whom does the curry belong? The entire goal of this book is to regain the public's and government's support in order to save the curry industry from imminent collapse, not to down play or criticise non-Tamil efforts on British soil or elsewhere.

Before we consider this further, let's revisit what we discussed in earlier chapters.

- Curry is a Tamil word that entered the English language in the 16th century through Portuguese and we have seen that this was when Portuguese was in full control of the islets, that previously belonged to the Jaffna Tamil Kingdom. Also, we discussed that the Tamil language is the world's oldest.

- We have also seen that the English East India Company which was incorporated in the 17th Century, 31st December 1600, started trading with the Indian subcontinent in the mid-17th century just after the English Civil War.

- In 1757, Robert Clive, one of the founders of 'British India' marched his troops from Madras, the state capital of today's Tamil Nadu, now known as Chennai, to Calcutta in Bengal to fight off the local ruler and the French at the battle of Plassey and with the nationalisation of the East India Company in 1858, British India was formed as a legal entity in the 19th century. The Tamil Muslim chefs that the British troops brought with them from Madras extended the curry (pre-Chilli era) to Bengal.

- Curry, as we've already seen, followed the British as they spread their colony throughout the subcontinent from Bengal. This is consistent with the claim made by some

Curry heritage of the Tamils

British authors that curry was introduced to India by the British, a claim we now know to be technically correct but misleading. The first curry house (Hindustani Coffee House) in London was founded by a Bengali in 1810 who arrived in the UK in 1784.

These facts reveal that the Tamil word 'Curry', which entered the English language in the 16th century, and the term 'Indian Curry', which first appeared in the 20th century, are therefore unrelated. Agree? We'll talk about this again shortly.

Further research will show that other food terms, like 'Poppadum', a popular item with curry lovers, is also from the Tamil language too.

Let's take a few more food-related items from the Tamil language. There is Mulligatawny. Millaku (Tamil word for Black Pepper) and Tawny(r) (Tamil word for Water –Tawny – informal word) are spelled together as Mulligatawny (Black Pepper Tonic or soup). Note that the correct wording for Mulligatawny is Millakuththawny (Millaku-th-thawny).

A simplified version of Millakuththanny is Rasam. Rasam, mostly herb based and intended to treat heartburn, indigestion, etc. Given that there was no western medicine (allopathy) available, these traditional Tamil remedies must have been popular among European colonists.

Congee (or Kanji) is another widely used Tamil food. It's just porridge, really (e.g. Rice Congee or Rice Porridge). This was an ancient food of the Tamils, especially the poor peasants.

It is noteworthy that, Curry, Poppadum, Mulligatawny, Rasam, Congee and Mango are all food related Tamil words used today by English speakers as well as that some of the words came via the Portuguese language.

Catamaran, Cash, Anicut, and Coir are some of the nonfood related Tamil words in English. We'll look more at all this in the next chapter.

CHAPTER 7

Recalling the History of the Tamils and their Language

We have discussed how black pepper was used in the mummification process of Egyptian pharaoh Ramesses II, providing evidence of the black pepper trade dating back at least 3200 years. This historical context highlights the long-standing importance of spices like black pepper in various cultures and trade routes.

Indeed, Tamil history is incredibly ancient and rich. We've touched upon the history of the three Tamil dynasties, including the Pandiyas with their capital in Madurai, one of the oldest recorded cities that continues to be vibrant today. The recent excavations at the Keeladi archaeological site near Madurai along the Vaikai River have been significant in shedding light on this ancient and culturally rich region.

The excavation at the Keeladi archaeological site, revealing an ancient Tamil civilization dating back to the 6th century BCE to the 1st century CE, has indeed been a treasure trove of history. It is noteworthy for establishing the existence of a civilization even older than the Sangam era.

The Sangam era, which spanned from 600 BCE to 200 CE, was a period in Tamizhakam (the Tamil region in the southern tip of the Indian subcontinent) when it was ruled by three Tamil dynasties - the Pandiyas, Cholas, and Cheras (who were believed to be princely siblings at one time), along with various independent chieftains known as the Velir. This era was known for its rich literary works, art, and culture, and the recent Keeladi findings have provided new insights into this ancient period. The ancient Tamil literature is classified into three specific periods known as the Sangam periods.

"Sangam" refers to a special occasion of gathering of nobles, often for the purpose of publishing their linguistic works. Sangam panel reviewed and either approved or rejected a work base on quality. Thus, a large number of ancient Tamil literary and poems categorised in accordance with their time of publication.

There were three Sangam periods, according to Tamil legends: Head Sangam(Sangam Period 1), Middle Sangam (Sangam Period 2), and Last Sangam(Sangam Period 3). These three periods correspond between 600 BC and AD200.

The Sangam literature is thought to have been produced by the academies of each period. The evidence of the early history of the Tamil kingdoms consists of the epigraphs of the region, the Sangam literature, and archaeological data.

Europeans and Curry are mentioned in these ancient writings. There are many literary works, and one of them is the more than 2000-year-old poem Thiru-Kural by the distinguished poet and sage Tiruvalluvar (Thiru-Valluvar), which has been translated into more than forty different languages including English and French.

The Rev. Dr. G.U. Pope was the first to translate Thiruk-kural into English. Many other translators followed.

The Thirukkural, which is often referred to as the Kural, is an impressive old Tamil text. Thiruvalluvar, a Tamil poet and philosopher, authored 1,330 little couplets or lyrics for it. The Thirukkural addresses many facets of life, including as morality, love, ethics, and governance.

The Thirukkural is especially notable because of its many translations and broad influence. It is still one of the most translated pieces of traditional Tamil literature, having been translated into several Indian as well as foreign languages. This illustrates the ageless wisdom and universal themes found in its lyrics, which elevate the work to a sacred status in both Tamil culture and the annals of world literature.

You can see a few of his ancient masterpieces in this book and those who travel on the Paris Metro system can see the French-translated poems in some compartments. There are a few of the 1330 couplets from 2000 years ago that discuss food consumption that are still valid today and may be of interest to dieters.

Let's take a look at half a dozen of them.

Couplet 942

மருந்து என்பது தேவைப்படாதாம்
உடம்பிற்கு உண்பதையும் செரிப்பதையும்
ஆராய்ந்து போற்றி உண்டால்.

In English

No need for medicine to heal your body's pain, If what you ate before is digested well, before you eat again.

Explanation:

If food is eaten eagerly, respectfully, and only after the previous meal has been digested well, the body wouldn't need anything referred to as medicine.

Couplet 943

செரிக்கும் அளவை அறிந்து உண்ண வேண்டும்.
அதுவே உடம்பு பெற்ற துயரத்தை அழிக்கும் வழி.

In English:

Who has a body gained may long the gift retain, If food digested well, in measure due he would eat again.

Explanation:

The best way to extend the life of an embodied soul is to eat in moderation and if (one's) food has been digested fully.

Couplet 944

செரிக்கும் அளவை அறிந்து கடைப்பிடித்து
ஒவ்வாமை தராத உணவை உண்க நன்கு பசித்ததும்.

In English:

Knowing the food digested well, when hunger prompted thee, With constant care, the viands choose that well.

Explanation:

Ensure that your food has been properly digested before you eat anything that is not disagreeable (to you) when you are extremely hungry.

Couplet 945

மனதிற்கும் உடலுக்கும் மாறுபாடு இல்லாமல்
விருப்பமான உணவாக இருப்பினும் அளவிற்கு
அதிகமாகாமல் மறுத்து அளவுடன் உண்டால் எவ்வித
தொல்லையும் இல்லை உயிர்க்கு.

In English:

With self-denial take the well-selected meal; So shall they frame no sudden sickness?

Explanation:
If one consumes food that is not disagreeable and in moderation, there won't be any danger to one's life.

Couplet 946

தேவைக்கு அதிகமாக எடுப்பது இழிவானது என்பதை அறிந்து உண்பவர் இடத்தில் நிலைத்து நிற்கும் இன்பம் போல் கட்டுப்பாடற்று உண்பவர் இடத்தில் நிலைக்கும் நோய்.

In English:
On modest temperance as pleasures pure, so pain attends the greedy epicure.

Explanation:
Similar to how pleasure resides with a moderate eater, disease resides with a voracious eater.

Couplet 947

தீயை எப்படி அளவுடன் பயன்படுத்துவது என்று அறியாதவர் போல் அளவற்று உண்பதால் நோயும் அளவற்று ஏற்படும்.

In English:
Who largely feeds, nor a measure of the fire within maintains, That thoughtless man shall feel unmeasured pains.

Explanation:
The fire that cooks our food can be dangerous if it is out of control, and the same is true for someone who consumes food in excess and is unaware of and is unaware of proper

health practises.

Centuries later, another renowned Tamil poet, often fondly referred to as Granny Avvai, took note of Thiruvalluvar's commendable work and the above related to food. However, realizing that his teachings were presented poetically and might require some time to fully grasp, she decided to encapsulate his wisdom into a brief and simple phrase:

'Pasiththup Pusi' (பசித்துப் புசி) : **'Consume food only when you are genuinely hungry'.**

***

Let me draw the threads together!

The word 'curry' was used to refer to black pepper in Sangam period literature. However, today it also refers to a variety of side dishes such as Kuzhampu (runny curry), pirattal (dry curry), sothi (white curry), lentils (white curry), spinach (white curry), and fish kuzhambu. All are commonly eaten with rice or other items made out of rice flour. Such dishes are also called 'curry' in English and other world languages today.

It is a word that went from Tamil to English in the 16th century via Portuguese.

The original 'curry', however, is a staple food in the daily diet of Tamils. This 'curry' refers to food that is cooked (cooked as curry) normally by boiling.

Okay, we have discussed already that curries can be classified into two types. One is vegetarian food (Saivam).

The other is non-vegetarian food (Asaivam).

Non-vegetarian food refers to meat as well as seafood dishes. There is also the case of calling it 'macha-curry'. (Macham refers to non-veg of seafood or meat.) Vegetarianism refers to foods derived from trees, plants, vines, etc. The term "mara-curry" in Tamil makes sense as it refers to plant-based curry. The word "maram" in Tamil means "plant," so "mara-curry" essentially translates to "plant-based food" or a curry primarily made from vegetables or plant-based ingredients.

This distinction makes it easier to recognise curries that are vegetarian or vegan and don't include any meat or animal products. It's a useful term for those who follow plant-based diets or need to identify such dishes when choosing from a menu or preparing a meal.

The term "curry-amuthuu," used by some Tamils to refer to "mara-curry" (plant-based curry), is a beautiful expression. "Curryamuthuu" essentially means "heavenly curry" or "food given by nature." This term reflects a deep appreciation for plant-based dishes and acknowledges the natural goodness of these curries. It's a testament to the rich cultural and culinary traditions in Tamil cuisine, emphasizing the connection between nature and food.

We have seen that in Sangam period literature, the word "curry" is also used to refer to pepper.

'Akananuru' (Tamil: அகநானூறு), a classical Tamil poetic work, is the seventh book in the anthology of Sangam literature (600 BCE - 300 CE),namely 'Ettuthokai' (a collection of eight volumes). In verse 149, it offers this poetic description:

"The fine ships of Yavanas, came cruising (from the Arabian sea) into the Sulli river, thereby making its white

Curry heritage of the Tamils

foam muddied, to barter curry (black pepper and other spices) with gold at the Musiri Town of Cheran (King of Chera dynasty)".

Historians agree that the word 'Yavanas' was used in ancient literature to refer to the Roman and Greek traders who came for spices. Remember that the Romans who ruled Britain between 45–440 CE also ruled Egypt between 333BCE – 646 CE. So technically curry (pepper) must have come to Britain first, during the Roman time.

Curry has been used in many places in the Sangam literature to refer to pepper (at least twenty two times in poems). The word (black) pepper is used only four times.

Here, I only copy the lines where the words 'curry' and 'pepper' appear and translate them into English. What is in bold are the names of the collections and the poem number followed by the line number. Note that these lines are part of poems describe a story.

(By the way, if you are interested in more details please check Appendix 2)

1. Curry (Pepper) vine spreading on sandalwood tree - **Akananuru 2-6**
2. Mountain where Curry (Pepper) – wine Spread - **Akananuru 112-14**
3. The yavanas (of Greeks and Romans) came in with gold and goods on board to barter curry (pepper) - **Akananuru 149-10**
4. An old deer with a roaring voice did not want to eat curry vine (pepper) **Akananuru 182-14**
5. Curry (Pepper) vines spread on the rock - **Akananuru 272-10**
6. On the hill where the pepper grows - **Nattinai 151-7**
7. The Peacock sleeping on grown up curry vines - **Nattinai 151- 7**
8. Pepper growing Hill - **Kurumthokai 90-2**
9. Pepper growing Hill - **Kurumthokai 288-1**
10. Hills where–pepper grows - **Five Hundred 243-1**
11. Pepper growing Mountain – Black Stone - **Ainkurunooru 246-1**
12. On the hill where the–pepper grows - **Kalithokai 52-17**

13. Rice cooked with curry (pepper) and meat - **Purananuru 14-14**
14. Pepper growing hill - **Purananuru 168-2**
15. Sacks of curry (pepper) that have been piled up in the houses - **Purananuru 343-3**
16. Sandalwood and pepper in the mountains - **Paripadal 16-2**
17. Clustered green pepper - **Malaipadukadam 521**
18. The clusters of Pepper hanging in the vine – **Thirumurukaartuppadai 309**
19. Pepper vines spread on –he jack tree - **Panattupadai 43**
20 Pomegranate pearls mixed with butter and pepper - **Perumpanatuppadai 307**
21. Ginger, turmeric, green–pepper, etc. - **Maduraikkanchi 289**
22. The sacks and sacks of black curry (pepper) that were unloaded and were carried by men - **Pattinapalai 186**

Ancient trading between Greeks, Romans, and Tamils

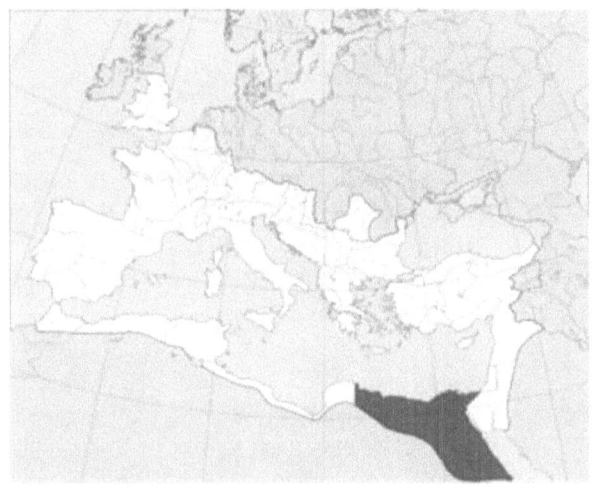

Aegyptus province in Egypt during the Roman time

The Ancient Greeks were the first to introduce pepper to Europe. Following Egypt's conquest by Alexander the

Great in 331 BCE, the Greeks adopted the Egypt custom of utilising pepper in sacred ceremonies.

Pepper was also used for medicinal purpose by the Greeks. Gradually they started using it for food seasonings. The Roman love for pepper as a seasoning and flavouring began when they started ruling Egypt, which led to a boom in demand for pepper under the Roman empire (333 BCE – 646 CE).

It is significant that over 80% (400 of the 500) recipes in the Roman cookbook Apicius of 900 CE contained pepper as one of its ingredients.

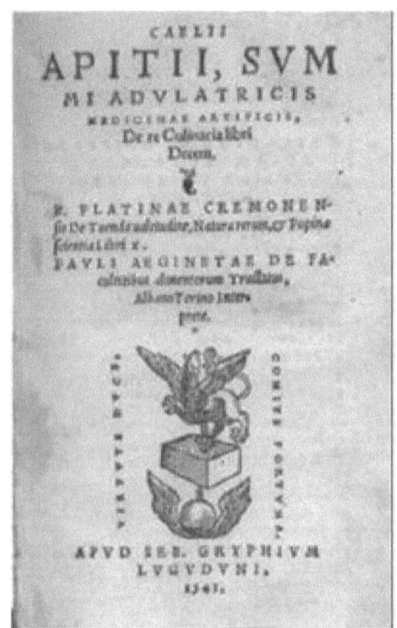

Roman cookbook

Remember too, about what we have seen in the literature of the Sangam periods. After these periods, there were five great epics of Tamil Literature came out and they are *Silappatikaram, Manimekalai, Cheevaka Cintamani, Valayapathi,* and Kundalakesi.

In the first, Silappatikaram, there are extensive references to Yavanas who arrived in Tamil Country as traders, guards of Tamil Kings' palaces, and soldiers in the Kings' army. This was possible because the Tamil country was rich from the spices and other items it was selling.

The book, Yavana Raani (Queen of Yavana)

Based on these historical facts and some fiction, there was a very popular Tamil novel 'Yavana Rani' (Queen of Yavana) authored by 'Sandilyan' which came out in the 20th century.

Pattinappalai, (Tamil: பட்டினப்பாலை) is another Tamil poetic work in the Pathi-nenmael-kanakku (means, 'volume of 10 chapters') anthology of Tamil literature, belonging to the Sangam period 1, corresponding to between 1st century BCE and 5th century BCE.

The ancient Chola port city of Kaveri-poom-pattinam (Poom-Puhar), which was situated at the mouth of the Kaveri River on the east coast, is vividly described in Pattinappaalai. The poet vividly talks of the thriving sea trade, the antics of Yavanas; the merchants from ancient Greece and Rome, their living quarters, etc. Additionally, it stated that this port city imports food to the Chola nation from Eelam (the Tamil region of the island of Eelam (nowadays Sri Lanka).

These vivid descriptions are so true to life that one might start to question if they are firsthand accounts rather than poetic creations. They offer intricate insights into the commodities traded through the Poom-Puhar port and the flourishing industries in the region.

Additionally, Pattinappalai provides an idealised description of the traders operating in PoomPuhar (Pattinappalai II - 199-212).

The ancient Tamil port city of Poompuhar was visited by large ships, according to Purananuru (Tamil: புறநானூறு), another piece of ancient Tamil literature from the same era. It was unfortunate that this port town along with Kaveri-poom-pattinam (Poom Puhar) submerged into the sea, either by tsunami or by rising sea level.

At the same time, trade also occurred along Cheras' west coast, primarily in Musiri Port; this was the coast where the Portuguese landed first in 1498 CE. The primary port city for the Pandyas was called Korkai.

Pompeii Lakshmi

The Pompeii Lakshmi is an ivory statuette that was discovered in the ruins of Pompeii, which was destroyed in the eruption of Mount Vesuvius in 79 CE. She was unearthed by an Italian scholar Amedeo Maiuri, in 1938.

The statuette has been dated to the first century of the Christian Era. The statuette is thought of as representing a Hindu goddess of feminine beauty, wealth, and fertility.

Lakshmi is a reminder of the commercial trade of goods and resources between the Indian subcontinent and Italy (Romans) in the first century. Over the years historians have been able to connect Roman trade with the Far East, specifically the Indian subcontinent.

There is an ancient papyrus Trade Agreement document written in Greek between Tamil and Greek merchants in 2 CE. It is now in the Vienna Museum.

Ancient papyrus trade agreement

A written contract for the delivery of goods from Musiri, an ancient Tamil port city, to Alexandria has been found in a museum in Vienna. Even though the contract itself is not in Tamil, the fact that it is entirely in Greek demonstrates how well-versed in the language the Tamil traders were.

Literary Sources

The Greeks and Romans are referred to as Yavanas in Sangam literature. The trade activities of Greek and Roman traders in the Tamil nation are described in the Sangam poems. They mentioned about imports and exports as well as important seaports.

The Greek and Roman authors of that time period also mentioned the specifics of the trade relations between their nations and the Tamil area. Specifically, authors like Pliny and Ptolemy. Plutarch and the author of the Periplus described the condition of trade in the first and second centuries of the

Christian era.

The archaeological evidence has further supplemented literary sources relating to foreign trade, The Arikamedu excavations remain important evidence for Greek and Roman trade in the Tamil country. Greeks and Romans continued to use Arikkamedu, a location close to Pondicherry, as a significant trade hub. There was a large Roman factory at Arikamedu, which the Greek authors had referred to as Poduke. There have also been numerous items discovered there, including coins, porcelain, jars, and tubs for dying clothing.

Other regions of Tamil Nadu have also yielded Roman coins, pottery, and other artifacts. Other locations that have had excavations done include Puhar, Kanchipuram, Alagankulam, Madurai, and Kodumanal. Coins from Greece and Rome as well as other artefacts have been discovered in these locations, supporting the Sangam Age's foreign trade.

Roman coins have been discovered all over Tamil Nadu, but especially in the coastal regions. We learn from these coins that Roman emperors like Augustus Caesar, Tiberius, and Nero had issued them. Due to the fact that these monarchs ruled between the first and second centuries CE, it may be stated that the Sangam era Tamils had commercial ties with the Roman Empire.

The Greeks were indeed among the first Europeans to establish trade contacts with the Tamil region around the third century BCE. They adopted and mentioned several Tamil names for the commodities available in the Tamil country. This historical interaction between the Greeks and the Tamils contributed to the exchange of goods, culture, and knowledge between the two regions.

For example, the Greeks used the term "Oriza" to refer to the Tamil word "Arici," which means rice. The Greeks paid significant attention to the west coast due to its proximity. Their primary trading hub continued to be the seaport of Musiri on the west coast of the Tamil region. Through their trade connections with Egypt, the Greeks established a crucial link between the western world and the Tamil nation.

The Romans followed the Greeks into the Tamil regions and initially engaged in trade with the Pandyan kingdom. They employed skilled merchants to buy and sell goods in local markets, and some of them even served in the Pandyan army. During the first and second centuries CE, Greek and Roman traders expanded their trade activities in the Tamil region. However, international trade gradually decreased after that period. The contacts between the Greek and Roman traders and the Tamil nation came to an end due to the turmoil within the Roman Empire and the conclusion of the Sangam era in the third century AD.

Exports and Imports

Throughout the Sangam Period, the Tamil nation exported a wide range of goods to Greece and Rome. Spices like ginger, cardamom, cinnamon, cloves, and pepper were among the most significant of them. Sandal paste, flowers, fragrances, aromatic wood like Ahil, ivory, pearls, corals, medicinal plants, bananas, salt, silk, and rice are some of the other exports.

Additionally, there was a significant market in the west for cotton clothing (muslin) made in the Tamil nation. Fine varieties of clothing had been exported to the West, according to Sangam literature. The Romans also purchased different kinds of beads, diamonds, sapphires, topaz, emeralds, and tortoise shells. The horses for the Pandyan and other South Indian kingdoms were imported via ships from other nations. The trained elephants were exported.

The Greeks introduced oil lamps and 'Paavai Vilakku' (statues of girls carrying lamps) to the Tamils, who were previously using flaming torches made of balls of oiled cotton on a stick for lighting. Jewellery of the Roman era such as 'Kasu Malai' or 'Garland of Gold Coins' is still popular among the Tamils.

The seaports located on the coasts of the Tamil nation made it simple for international trade to develop. During the Sangam era, Tamil Nadu had a number of seaports. On the eastern coast, Mamallapuram, Poduke, Puhar, Poraiyaru, Korkai, and Kumari were the most significant.

Details about the Puhar harbour and its activities are provided in the Sangam literature, Pattinappalai. The port city of Korkai had continued to be well-known for its pearls. It served as the Pandyan kingdom's main port. Musiri and Thondi were the two major seaports on the west coast.

Along the coasts, warehouses for storing the goods were constructed.

The major ports had their own lighthouses, which Tamil literature refers to as "Kalangarai Ilangu Sudar". Additionally, facilities for ship repairs were built in the seaports. During the Sangam era, foreign merchants frequently visited and stayed in port towns. Port towns were home to residents from many different nations, which facilitated the growth of a cosmopolitan civic structure there.

Thus, the Tamil nation maintained trade and other contacts with Greece and Rome throughout the Sangam period. The ports of modern-day Yemen are thought to have served as the hub of trade for Yavanas, Romans, Greeks, and Arabs at that time.

The Tamils' social, economic, religious, and cultural lives

were profoundly impacted by the Sangam Age in their homeland. The Sangam period saw numerous developments. These developments date back to very early times, when the Tamil nation engaged in extensive trade with other nations, according to both the Sangam literature and archaeological discoveries.

Beginning around the third century BCE, the Greeks and Romans kept up trade relations with the Tamil nation. These business ties persisted throughout the Sangam era. The Sangam Age's maritime activities can be studied using a variety of sources.

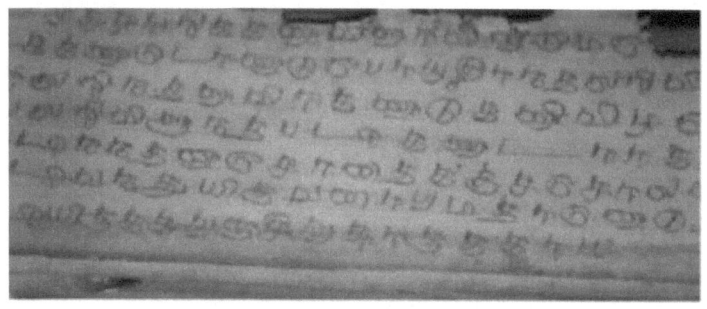

Ancient Palm Leaf manuscript in Tamil

The Romans were dominant in Egypt from 30 BCE to 641 CE and in England between 43 and 410 CE. Therefore, technically, curry and especially black pepper must have arrived in Britain during the Roman era, which was centuries before the 16th century, when the word curry entered the English language, according to the Oxford Dictionary. In other words, the word 'curry' was likely in use in Britain even before the English language was developed.

The first European trade link persisted in various ways throughout the first millennium but came to an end with the start of the second millennium, specifically at the start of the

Middle Ages (1095–1492 CE) when the Crusades began, which barred Europeans from accessing the Mediterranean Sea. However, the Arabs had exclusive access to the Arabian and Mediterranean during these times, giving them a competitive advantage in the spice trade.

The second European trade link with the Tamils was established toward the end of the Middle Ages with Vasco da Gama's visit in May 1498. It should now be evident that, contrary to the claims of many authors, Vasco da Gama was not the first European to have visited the Tamils for trade.

I will discuss the 2017 Chinese excavation activities on my islet shortly. According to the Chinese, there was a commercial centre there just before the Middle Ages. In conclusion, my islet served as a hub for traders from China, the Arab world, Portugal, the Netherlands, and the United Kingdom. The last three were colonisers.

Tamils and–the Far East - The Chola Empire

Chera, Chola, and Pandya were the three ancient Tamil dynasties that we have already explored. (Cheras are now referred to as Malayalees speaking Malayalam, a language that branched off from Tamil.)

The Cholas were the most powerful among these three dynasties, and they expanded their kingdom overseas. According to ancient Tamil writings, the Chola kingdom never suffered from a rice shortage. This suggests the presence of a highly advanced irrigation system that allowed for rice cultivation three times a year.

In Cheevaka Cintamani, one of the five Tamil epics, it is described how families would stand outside and invite pilgrims to their homes to share rice and curries with them. Those who accepted the invitation would also be offered gifts, such as silk clothing. This provides insight into the way people lived during that period and their hospitality customs.

The world's first anicut (dam) was initially constructed by King Karikalan of the Chola Dynasty between 100 and 150 CE, and the British restored it in the 19th century.

At the time that William the Conqueror, the duke of Normandy, invaded England in the 11th century AD, the Chola Emperor Rasa-Rasan (King of the Kings), was expanding his kingdom by dispatching naval forces to Java and Sumatra (both in Indonesia), as well as a portion of Kadara (Malasiya). Today, Bali became the only region of Indonesia to remain predominantly Hindu (Saiva).

Hindus make up the majority of the population of the island off Bali's east coast, and there are other Hindu settlements close to Java's eastern beaches. These are the results of the Chola Empire's expansion.

The Cholas kept diplomatic and commercial ties with Vietnam, Cambodia, Laos, and Thailand (Siam).

The Cholas dispatched diplomats and Tamil traders to the Khmer Empire of Cambodia, China, and Thailand. (The Cholas contributed to the accomplishment of Angkor Wat's completion. The largest Hindu temple in the world is Angkor Wat).

Angkor Wat - World's largest Hindu Temple

Curry heritage of the Tamils

Tamils and Thailand

The sea trade between ancient Thailand and Tamil Nadu is well documented. A few Brahmin priests were dispatched to the court of Thailand's kings by the Chola dynasty king as a result of the Chola's strong influence in that country. Even today, priests would chant hymns in Tamil and Sanskrit during a coronation ceremony, continuing this tradition.

Though the link was ancient, a sizeable Tamil population has been in Thailand since 1860, with the majority of them being members of the Tamil merchant society known as "Chettiars". Chola Links, Portuguese presence, and then 'Tamil Chettiars' migrations and also the curry culture among the Tamils in nearby Malaysia helped the Thai curry culture to flourish. This 'Chola period' is considered a 'glorious era' of the Tamils.

Lord Shiva's Temple, also named 'Peru Udayar temple' was built in the 11th century, by Chola emperor Rasa Rasan in Tanjore, the Chola Empire's capital in the south Indian sub-continent (currently Tamil Nadu in India). The temple is a part of the UNESCO World Heritage Site known as the 'Great Living Chola Temples'. Today, it attracts many visitors and pilgrims from all over the world.

The Tamil merchants themselves built a Shiva temple in Chuan Chou, China. According to Ms. Wang of the Quanzhou Maritime Museum, the oldest record of Tamil inhabitants of Quanzhou dates back to the seventh century.

The Kaiyuan Temple was originally constructed in the Tang Dynasty between 685 and 686 CE, but it was restored and dedicated to Lord Shiva by the Tamil Hindu merchant community in the city in the late 13th century.

It is believed the Chola kings had thriving trade relations with South East Asia including China. At that time, the Bay of Bengal was referred to a "Chola Lake."

We've discussed the rich historical connections of the Tamil Merchant community known as the Chettiars and their involvement in trade with various regions, including China. This history has contributed to the development of various curry styles, such as pre-chilli era Thai Curry, Vietnam Curry, and Chinese curry, which later evolved into post-chilli era curry, influenced by Portuguese and French interactions as discussed earlier. These diverse culinary influences are a testament to the global reach of Tamil curry traditions.

The Chola Empire and Eelam

A military invasion of the Kingdom of Anuradhapura by the mighty Chola Empire resulted in the conquering of Sri Lanka and taking over the Anuradhapura Kingdom.

It initially began with the invasion of the Anuradhapura Kingdom in 993 AD by RasaRasa I when he sent a large Chola army to conquer the kingdom and absorb it into the Chola Empire.

Most of the island was subsequently conquered by 1017 and incorporated as a province of the vast Chola empire during the reign of his son Rajendra Chola.

Chola areas in Polonnaruwa were called 'Jagannatha Mandalam'. (Remember Curry Mandalam (Coromandel).

Curry in the Bible

The spices of the Tamils and King Solomon were mentioned in the Bible. In some ancient Tamil works of literature, the word Curry is also referring to Spices.

Queen of Sheba ascending the court of King Solomon

The reference to the Queen of Sheba in the Bible underscores the historical trade connections between ancient Israel and the kingdom of Saba (Sheba) in southwest Arabia, specifically Ethiopia in some historical interpretations. The account in the biblical narrative describes her journey to the court of King Solomon, leading a camel caravan laden with valuable items, including gold, jewels, and spices. The presence of spices in her offerings reflects the importance of spices in ancient trade, and the biblical text notes that "Never again came such an abundance of spices," emphasizing the significance of this trade connection. (10:10;II Chron. 9:1–9).

The story of the Queen of Sheba's visit to King Solomon, as told in the Bible, does indeed include her posing riddles and testing Solomon's wisdom. Her gifts, which included valuable spices, undoubtedly piqued the king's interest. Given the historical trade connections and the abundance of spices in the region, it's quite plausible that these spices were sourced from the Tamils regions across the Arabian Sea. Spices have been a significant part of international trade for centuries, and the ancient trade routes, including those connecting the Arabian Peninsula and the Indian subcontinent, facilitated the exchange of such valuable commodities.

Tamils and the Jews

The introduction of valuable spices by the Queen of Sheba likely did arouse interest in them, and it's fascinating to consider the historical connections between different regions and communities. The claim that King Solomon's merchants helped the Cochin Jews reach the Malabar coast of the Chera country is an interesting one. Trade and migration have long played significant roles in shaping the movement of people and cultures throughout history. Kerala, also known as Malabar, was indeed a notable region with a rich history, and it was part of the Chera dynasty's Tamil territory. These historical interactions and the exchange of goods and knowledge have left a lasting impact on the cultures and traditions of these regions.

The first Jewish settlements in the Indian sub-continent were located in the Cochin Kingdom within modern-day Kerala, the land of the Chera dynasty of the Tamils. It is said that traders from Israel arrived in Cranganore, an ancient port near Cochin, in 562 BC, and more Jews were exiled from Israel in 70 AD after the Second Jerusalem Temple was destroyed.

According to several of these Jews' ancestors; they arrived in the Indian subcontinent during the reign of the Hebrew King Solomon. During this period, trade in Cochin was mostly focused on teak wood, ivory, spices, monkeys, and peacocks.

Many of these Jewish immigrants were skillful craftsmen

too and they were making jewellery and ornaments for the womenfolk in the palaces and the riches of the 'spice rich' kingdoms of the Tamils. Following expulsion from Iberia in 1492 by the Alhambra Decree of Spain, many Jews arrived in Tamil areas including Chennai (Madras).

In 52 CE, Saint Thomas and the Arab Jews from Syria travelled to Nagercoil and the Kanyakumari District (in present-day Tamil Nadu state of India). The majority of them were business people who had settled close to Thiruvithamcore. The neighbouring ports of Colachel and Thengapattinam enabled them to preserve commercial ties with Europe in the early days, and their language skills were useful to the Travancore Kings to communicate with other European traders and merchants.

There were other Jewish communities in Mumbai and Goa (the Portuguese colony). When Portuguese Princes married King Charles II of England, Bombay was given as a dowry.

The close association between the Cochin Jews and Tamil kings, as inscribed through copper plates known as 'Sasanam' in Tamil, provided the Jewish community with exceptional privileges and recognition.

Rabbi Salmon Halevi and his wife Rebecca in Madras, capital of the state of Tamil Nadu during British colonial period

These copper plates with edicts, presented to them by Bhaskara Ravi Varma, the fourth Malabar king, granted the Jews rights and control over the village of Anjuvannam, with an enduring legacy that extended 'as long as the world and moon exist.'

For more than a millennium, the Jews lived in peace within Anjuvannam, enjoying the privileges and protection afforded by the copper plates. However, the intervention of neighboring princes led to the revocation of these privileges during Rabban's rule, leaving the Jewish community without the same protection and rights they once enjoyed. This historical account reflects the shifting dynamics of power and the complexities of interactions between various communities and rulers in the region.

The arrival of the Portuguese and the consequences on the Jews

We have already discussed that Vasco da Gama was not received well by the Zamorin king and on his way out, he and his team were attacked by the Arab Muslim traders who were in the harbour area.

After the Portuguese arrival in 1498, the Arab Muslim traders assaulted the Jews under the false pretence that they were disrupting their business in spice by assisting the Portuguese in their journey from Europe. Their homes and synagogues were also destroyed.

One possible reason for this is the arrival of many Jewish refugees in 1492 due to the Alhambra Decree in Spain, followed by the Portuguese in 1498. It is likely that some of these Jewish individuals served as translators between the Portuguese and the Zamorin King and his courtiers. This may have raised suspicions.

However, it's important to note that the Jews arrived via the Mediterranean and Arabian seas, while the Portuguese arrived after circumnavigating Africa.

"Malabarese Jews", as depicted by the Portuguese in the 16th century

In the aftermath of the Portuguese expulsion that followed their arrival in 1498, Arab Muslim traders who opposed them also targeted the Jewish community. They falsely accused the Jews of interfering with the black pepper trade by aiding the Portuguese in their journey from Europe. As a result, the Jews had their homes and synagogues destroyed.

The damage was so extensive that when the Portuguese returned a few months later with more firepower and established themselves in the Cochin area of Kerala, only a small number of impoverished Jews remained. The Malabar Jews have a synagogue and a cemetery at Mala, Thrissur District, as well as in Chendamangalam, Parur, and Ernakulam.

Even though they are no longer being used for their original purpose, Kerala still has at least seven synagogues. There are now very few Jews, and many of them moved to

Israel after 1948.

In neighboring Ceylon, Sir Sidney Solomon Abrahams PC QC (11 February 1885 – 14 May 1957), who served as the Chief Justice of the country from 1936 to 1939, had Jewish origins. Subsequently, many of these Jews from India and Sri Lanka relocated to Western countries and Australia after the end of British rule.

The Indian Prime Minister's visit to Israel in 2017

On July 3, 2017, while on a state visit to Israel, Indian Prime Minister Narendra Modi made the following statement in a speech: "Two thousand years ago, Jewish traders came to India to buy spices and our relationship was longstanding".

However, rather than referring to 'India,' which, as I mentioned, didn't exist as such 2000 years ago, the Prime Minister should have spoken of the Indian sub-continent or the Tamil lands, as India was formally established by the British many centuries later. But, in conclusion, the relationship between the Tamils and Jews is very long and has always been very cordial.

Chapter 8

Seeking Vikings in the Curry Lands

The love of Europeans for their spices – for 'their curry' – goes back a long way. Astonishingly, history records that the Vikings too fought for their curry. When I say "Vikings" here, I mean the maritime Norse pirates from southern Scandinavia (modern-day Denmark, Norway, and Sweden), who attacked, traded, and settled in several locations across Europe from the 8th to the 11th century.

The Vikings also travelled as far as the Mediterranean, North America, the Middle East, and North Africa. (The period when some of the nations they conquered and settled is known as the Viking Age, and the term "Viking" is frequently used to describe all of the inhabitants of the Norse homelands.).

The early medieval histories of regions such as Scandinavia, the British Isles, France, Estonia, and Kievan Rus were profoundly influenced by the Vikings. Known for their prowess in combat and their exceptional seafaring skills, as demonstrated through their iconic longships, the Vikings established Norse settlements and governance in numerous countries. These territories included Britain, Ireland, the Faroe Islands, Iceland, Greenland, Normandy, the Baltic coast, and extended to the Dnieper and Volga trade routes in what is now European Russia, Belarus, and Ukraine.

The Norse colonists contributed to the formation of the Norse-Gaels, Rus' people, Faroese, and Icelanders, and intermingled with the Anglo-Saxons. It's worth noting that the Vikings also made less-known voyages to places like Iran, Arabia, and Constantinople. Remarkably, they were the first Europeans to set foot in Newfoundland, Canada.

The Vikings not only exported their own culture but also introduced elements of foreign cultures, including slaves and concubines, to Scandinavia. Over time, the Norse homelands evolved from small kingdoms into the larger entities of Denmark, Norway, and Sweden. The Viking population was primarily composed of individuals engaged in various occupations, such as craftsmen, farmers, fishermen, and traders. Contrary to common stereotypes, archaeological and historical evidence highlights the complex and advanced nature of Viking culture, which often diverges from popular misconceptions.

But back to that little-known fact that the Vikings, particularly the Danish, came for the curry (spices) as well.

Since the third century BCE, the Coromandel Coast, known as the Curry Mandalam, had been a significant center for international trade. This coastal region had warehouses, lighthouses, and a bustling trade scene, primarily dealing with spices. Goods were transported by ox-driven carts, and barter was a common practice. Numerous Europeans, referred to as "Yavanas" or "Yavana Traders" in ancient Tamil literature, also frequented these areas. This historical context helps explain why the Vikings, including the Danish, may have been drawn to this region during their explorations.

By 1498, the Portuguese had arrived, then the Dutch, French, Danish, and lastly the British. They all colonised this region and established commercial ports there. In late 1530 the Coromandel Coast – the southeastern coastal region of the Indian subcontinent, bounded by the Utkal Plains to the north, the Bay of Bengal to the east, the Kaveri Delta to the south, and the Eastern Ghats to the west, extending over an area of about 22,800 square kilometers – was home to three Portuguese trading settlements at Nagapattinam, São Toméde Meliapore, and Pulicat.

The Dutch eventually established themselves at Pulicat, Sadras, and Covelong; the French in Pondicherry, Karaikal, and Nizampatnam; the British in Fort St.George (Madras) and Masulipatnam; and the Danish in Dansborg near Tharangambadi.

The confusion among local Tamils between the Danes and the Dutch is understandable, as the Danes are from Denmark, and the Dutch are from the Netherlands (Holland). However, distinguishing between them might have been challenging for many.

This confusion was likely compounded by the simultaneous arrival of both Dutch and Danish traders along the Curry Zone, which could have further perplexed the Tamils in distinguishing between the two groups.

It was around 1620 that the Danish admiral Ove Gjedde negotiated a contract with the local Tamil ruler Raghunathar of Tanjore allowing them to rent a 2.5-mile-square-mile territory. They built a fort known now as 'Fort Dansborg' at Tranquebar, now Tharangambadi.

Indeed, it's quite fascinating that this fort was the second-largest Danish fort globally, with Fort Kronborg in Helsingor being the only one surpassing it in size. Fort Dansborg was constructed in the distinct Danish architectural style, known for its expansive halls, columned buildings, tall ceilings, and projecting draperies. During the early 17th century, Fort Dansborg played a central role in Danish settlement efforts in the region.

Originally a fishing community, Tharangambadi (also known as Tranquebar) was used by the Danish as their principal commerce hub particularly to export cotton textiles and spices.

The fort served as a crucial crossing point for trade travelling to Europe from Coromandel. King Frederick IV, who was also the leader of the Danish Lutheran Church, despatched Protestant missionaries from Denmark.

The Tranquebar Mission was founded by two of them, Bartholomäus Ziegenbalg and Heinrich Plütschau, who arrived in Tranquebar on July 9, 1706, founded the fort and learned Tamil quickly. They also became the first to translate and print "The New Testament" of the Bible in Tamil using the fort's printing press. The Danish mission was the first **Protestant mission** in the Indian subcontinent.

The town's commercial prominence began to decrease in the middle of the 18th century, and Serampore, in the Bengal state, became the hub of textile manufacture. But the Danesh's head office remained in Tranquebar.

When the fort and the town were sold to the British in 1845, the fort along with Tharangambadi lost its importance because the town was no longer a trading hub. Today, the fort is a museum that has a variety of significant relics from both the fort and the Danish Empire and is one of the most popular tourist destinations in the area.

The Curry Mandalam or Curry Zone

Curry, as we know it now, is a Tamil word, and the Tamil word, Mandalam refers to an area, district, or zone. The Curry Mandalam or Curry Zone was a coastal region where foreigners had commercial posts and engaged in the import and export of cotton and spices. In the past, curry referred to spices, especially, the black pepper.

During the reign of the great Tamil Chola dynasty emperor RasaRasan (King of the Kings) of the 11th century, his territory was known as 'Chola Mandalam' and he used to name the overseas areas he conquered with a similar name. 'Jagannatha Mandalam', and 'Sathirvethi Mandalam' to name a few.

The Curry Mandalam (Coromandel Coast), which covers an area of about 22,800 square kilometers, is on the southeast coast of the Tamil region of the Indian subcontinent. The southwestern coast known as Malabar, which was the land of Cheras or modern-day Kerala, has been included in historical Muslim records as part of the Curry Mandalam (Coromandel Coast) from the 12th century.

The island of Ceylon's northwestern shore (one of the two Tamil habitats - the former Jaffna Tamil Kingdom) can also be seen as falling under this description of the 'curry zone'. You will see later the Chinese excavation activities in the largest islet in 2017, stating that they have a trading hub there.

Curiously, an Italian explorer by the name of Ludovico di Varthema may have used the name Curry Mandalam for the first time in 1510, and it appears that the Portuguese placed it on their maps after that.

However, it was the Dutch who started to do serious business there and gave it the name Coromandel. Like so many other instances, it seems that the Dutch had trouble pronouncing the term "Curry Mandalam" which is how the single word "Coromandel" came to be employed. Remember the word "Mulligatawny" (sic), which is still being referred to by Europeans as a single word rather than the two words it contains, "Milaku Tawny(r)"?

Along with Masoolipatnam, Pazhaverkadu (Pulicat, which was taken from the Portuguese) was an early Dutch settlement (trading posts) in southern India.

There is a Dutch fort and a cemetery belonging to the 17th century that is still at Pulicat. There were three Portuguese settlements on the Coromandel Coast by the end of 1530: Nagapattinam, São Tomé de Meliapore, and Pulicat. The Coromandel Coast was the scene of conflicts between European powers over control of the cotton and spice trades in the 17th and 18th centuries.

However, eventually, the British won out and Coromandel became part of British India, although France retained the tiny enclaves of Pondichéry and Karaikal until as late as 1954. Coromandel became part of the British Indian coast. From the Coromandel Coast, the British exported goods to Europe, China, Thailand, Japan, and other countries in the Far East.

Four ships of the Royal Navy have borne the name **HMS Coromandel** after the coastal area of the Tamils. The Coromandel Peninsula in New Zealand was named after one of these ships, and the town, 'Coromandel', is also on the peninsula.

It was the Coromandel ship, which brought 156 English settlers to Holdfast Bay from London in 1837, that gave the South Australian suburbs of Coromandel Valley and Coromandel East their names. Some of the crew members absconded after the ship had reached the shore with the intention of staying behind in South Australia and seeking safety in the hills of the Coromandel Valley area.

The name Indija Koromandija (also known as India Coromandel) refers to a region in Slovenia where it is said that the houses are 'bleached with cheese and covered with cake", making it a realm of prosperity, a promised land, and a paradise.

Recently, an excavation effort was carried out in the coastal area of another village, 'Allaipiddy' in the islet, where I was born and brought up, by a group of archaeologists from the Shanghai Museum in China, led by Chen Jie, to look for connections to the old silk route.

According to Chen Jie, the trade connection dates back to 2000 years ago, and archaeological findings have supported this claim as well as records from the literature. There have been several discoveries of Chinese ceramics, coins, and other artifacts.

As part of the excavations conducted by the Chinese archaeologists in Allaipiddy, a seaside village in the Tamil region of northern Sri Lanka, where the Chinese believe that they had a trading post, six hundred pieces of ancient Chinese pottery have been found, according to the Shanghai Museum.

Due to the fact that many Chinese products were consolidated at the Coromandel ports, boxes, screens, and chests made of lacquer became known as 'Coromandel' goods throughout the eighteenth century.

Excavation activities of Chinese in 'Allipiddy' – a coastal village in my islet in 2017

The Japanese and Korean dimensions

We have already hinted at the commercial relationship between Portugal and Japan. In fact, the whole 'Post-Chilli' era curry of the Tamils was introduced by the Portuguese to the Far East, including Thailand, Japan, and China. We saw earlier about the Post-Chilli era Japanese Katsu Chicken Curry being served successfully in the UK.

Let's now explore the Pre-Chilli Era Connections.

Professor Susumu Ohno of Gakushuin University in Japan puts it this way: "2000 years ago, during the Yayoi Period (500 BCE to 300 CE), the Tamils came to Japan to teach us how to plant, harvest, and consume rice. Professor Ohno has studied the relationship between the Japanese and Tamil languages. All this explains how Japanese rice and curry (pre-chilli era) came to be.

When a Japanese curry restaurant chain, **Coco Ichibanya**, opened its first outlet in New Delhi in 2019 it boasted it had reached its final destination, "the birthplace of curry"

Curry heritage of the Tamils

.The chain announced that their presence in India felt like their arrival at the "final destination", in the words of Tamotsu Nomura, director of Ichibanya India Pvt Ltd.

Such loose talk can be annoying to true curry lovers and to the Tamils too. Consider, for example, that in the UK, there are four nations and each nation has its own particular national dishes. Haggis, a savoury pudding containing sheep's pluck, minced with onion, oat meal, suet, spices, and salt, mixed with stock, and traditionally cooked while encased in the sheep's stomach is unique to Scotland.

If a foreign chain opened a Haggis restaurant in, let's say, Belfast, Northern Ireland, and announced that "we have reached our ultimate destination UK, the home of the Haggis", that would surely indicate that they lacked some awareness of the dish they serve, right?

This is my interpretation of Coco Ichibanya's assertion: they are unaware of the origins of the curry they offer, as well as the historical context of its introduction to Japan. I hope this book will provide the clarification they need. They are also likely unaware of Professor Susumu Ohno's work at Gakushuin University in Japan, as well as the historical connections between Portugal and Japan, including those related to curry. In any case, New Delhi has nothing to do with Curry but Chennai (Madras) and Jaffna do.

Tamils and their curry have existed for thousands of years in the island nation of Sri Lanka as well as in southern India; these two places were their natural habitats.

What about Korea, though? There's a story involving Kyugsoo Kim, a consular official for the Republic of Korea in Chennai (Madras), who was visiting a historical site in Mahabalipuram, Tamil Nadu, located near a beach close to Chennai.

The story goes that he turned to check whether his son

was there calling him when he heard the word 'Appa', the Tamil word for father, which is also used in Korean. He was shocked to discover that a child was calling out to his own father. This prompted Kyugsoo Kim to study the two languages and find out that they shared at least five hundred words.

How could this be? Well, it is believed that these two civilizations first interacted during the reign of King Suro and Ayi of the Pandyan Kingdom in CE 45.

There's a chance that Queen Huh (her post-marriage name), who traveled to Korea with many of her maids' families, brought Tamil culture with her.

So, thanks to Portuguese trading with the Far East, we can now savor curries with Korean influences.

Okay, I am sure we have gone through enough evidence of the pre-chilli and post-chilli eras of curry that span over three thousand two hundred long years. Let us now look into some related matters. Starting with another aspect of the Portuguese in Bengal.

The story begins with the powerful local Sultan permitting Portuguese trading activities in the Chittagong region (today an area of modern-day Bangladesh) during the 16th century.

The Chittagong settlement was unique among Portuguese settlements in that a significant portion of its residents were privateers. Portuguese privateers, freebooters, convicts, and adventurers were essentially unofficial settlers who arrived in this region with hopes of amassing their own wealth.

Among them were casados (married or retired military men), pirates, and individuals expelled from official Portuguese territories due to their misconduct. Consequently, they held less influence and had a relatively minor impact on the area. I'm discussing them because of their contributions to culinary development, including the possible creation of a distinctive beef curry.

Their presence is attributed to the development of a technique for producing curdled cheese, leading to the creation of Bandel cheese and the innovation of renowned sweet treats such as Sandesh and Rasgulla.

The Portuguese are credited with introducing several culinary elements to the subcontinent and the Chittagong region. They brought bread, chillis, and new vegetables to the area. Unlike the Hindu-majority Tamil territories where cows were considered sacred, the Chittagong region was mainly Muslim. This difference allowed for the consumption of beef, leading to the creation of the famous beef-based dish Kala bhuna, which remains popular in the region.

In the Portuguese colonies of northern Ceylon's Tamil region, cows played another significant role. They were used to fulfill tax obligations. Similar to how pepper was accepted for tax payments in medieval Europe, the people in these colonies were required to send cows to cover their tax dues or even to pay a ransom. Interestingly, the Portuguese consumed these cows.

When people chose to fulfill their tax obligations through means other than providing cows, it often resulted in raids on Hindu temples to steal milking cows. The Tamils were further agitated by the Portuguese practice of eating cows, which was not a part of the Tamil dietary tradition. This cultural clash added to the tension between the Tamils and the Portuguese.

This practice and the Portuguese' very aggressive policy of converting the locals to Catholicism annoyed the locals very much and so, eventually, the Dutch were able to replace the Portuguese quite easily. Under Dutch who followed

Protestantism, the Tamils enjoyed significant degree of religious freedom.

Dark Pork Padre Curry

Oh, did I forget to mention the 'Dark Pork Padre Curry' that the Portuguese left behind? The Portuguese word 'padre' denotes a priest. Dark Pork Padre (Priest) Curry was preferred by Catholic clergymen who came from Portugal to spread Christianity. The local hunters brought the wild boar meat for them, and they prepared curry with the newly innovated 'Curry Thuool'. We will see this recipe too.

I could continue discussing all this further. However, I am conscious this book is really about curry and so, in the next chapter, I will focus again much more precisely on that.

So let's again turn our attention to curry itself now.

Chapter 9

Giving Thanks to the Nature - The Thai Pongal Festival

The ancient Tamils understood that the Sun was the ultimate source of energy responsible for providing food to sustain all life on Earth. While other living beings consume what nature offers, humans have the unique ability to produce and choose their own food.

Pongal is a harvest festival that pays tribute to the Sun, which is the primary source of energy for food production. The festival typically spans three or even four days, with the second day dedicated to honoring the oxen that played essential roles in plowing the paddy fields and transporting the harvest to homes and markets.

Below are some messages from the Prime Ministers of the UK, Canada and very first time in 2023 from the Australian Prime Minster, marking the Tamils' Thai Pongal Day.

Please use your phone camera to scan the QR code **individually**.

The Tamil people observe Thai Pongal on January 14, which is the first day of Thai, the harvest month. (Or on January 15 in leap years). The Tamil calendar states that the Tamil New Year begins on the first day of the Tamil month of Chithhirai. Based on the Gregorian calendar, this month's first day is April 14. (April 15 in a leap year).

The Tamil word for the tenth month of the year is Thai (தை). Its literal translation is "Thanks giving Day of Tamils in the month of Thai." And it is on this day that the Tamil Curry Year begins.

The major reason Thai Pongal is observed is to thank the Sun for a good crop. One component of the ceremony involves boiling the first rice of the season and making a rice dish called Pongal that is dedicated to the Sun.

The harvest is completed early in January, and the paddy should arrive at home to be stored. If there is an abundance, the house is blessed because the family won't have to worry about food until at least the following harvesting cycle.

The paddy will be husked out and the new rice will be ready for Pongal day. On Pongal day, depending on where the morning sunlight comes first, usually, the porch, courtyard, or backyard will be decorated and a temporary fire place is a setup to prepare the Pongal.

The word 'Pongal,' literally means 'overflowing,' and signifies wealth and prosperity that is overflowing in the household. On the day of Pongal, milk is boiled in a pot, usually a brand-new clay pot, and when the milk starts to bubble and pour over the edge of the pot, fresh rice grains are added to the pot.

Along with rice and milk, this delicious dish also contains cashew nuts, cardamom, raisins, split green gram (Mung dhal), ghee, honey, and jaggery. As the dish is made in honour of the Sun, also known as Surya, Pongal begins just as the sun is about to rise, typically in the backyard, courtyard, or porch where the sunrise is visible.

Once the dish is ready, it is traditionally served on banana leaves and also with various fruits, offered to the sun as it comes out fully. Songs in praise of the sun are sung and then the household shares the dish and also with the neighbours.

Pongal has two variants, one is sweet as described above and the other is non-sweet. Those who don't like sweets, for whatever reason, will share this. A suitable vegetable curry is also made to complement this. In Sri Lanka, Tamils make Sambal for this non-sweet Pongal rice while in Tamil Nadu, Tamils make a vegetable soup known as Sambar.

A recipe will be seen later on, called Venn Pongal (White Pongal – remember; White Curries), which is a non-sweet Pongal dish. Following Pongal day, the harvested rice will be consumed throughout the year and excessive rice will be sent out to the market to be sold.

What's more, there are many varieties of rice dishes (as opposed to plain rice, eaten with various curries): Yoghourt Rice, Tomato Rice, Yellow Rice, Milk Rice, Lemon Rice, Tamarind Rice, Kathama Rice (Rice is cooked along with many vegetables, tamarind and curry powder; some call this as Vegetable Pongal.), Mixed Rice (Sautéed vegetable mixed with cooked rice), Chicken Rice, Seafood Rice, Mutton Rice, etc. We will see these recipes later which some find easy and quick to make.

Furthermore, rice flour, as opposed to wheat flour, is used to prepare breakfast and dinner items. Many curry enthusiasts who are familiar with rice and curries may not have had the chance to experience these renowned Tamil curry and food delicacies at their dinner tables, and it's a culinary experience not to be missed.

A few dishes that can be a part of Tamil curry traditions are pittu, hoppers, string hoppers, dosa, idly, roti, and koththu roti, as well as snacks (short eats) including fish cutlets, fish buns, mutton rolls, patties, bonda, vadai, and murukku.

Remember that Biriyani is not a dish of Tamils or even of India. It is an Arabian (Persian) dish that became popular in the northern part of the Indian subcontinent during the reign of the Mongol dynasty and spread southward during the British colonisation when the whole subcontinent became known as India. But the fact was the Arab traders who came to the Tamils for spices, also picked up an ancient recipe of the Tamils, the 'Uhoon Soru' (Meat Rice), and developed it as Biriyani.

Pongal is celebrated in the Indian state of Tamil Nadu, Union of Pondicherry (a separate Tamil habitat which was a French colony), and in the island of Sri Lanka, as well as by the Tamils living outside these areas, UK, Canada, US, Australia, New Zealand, Malaysia, Singapore, and many other countries.

The month in which Pongal, or the harvesting festival is celebrated, in January and it is now recognised as **'Tamil Heritage Month'** by many governments and local bodies such as the **Greater London Authority**, the **Government of Canada**, and **the State of Washington, Provincial Government of Ontario** – to name just a few.

As mentioned earlier, the word 'Pongal' means overflowing. Overflowing means, overflowing in all aspects of life: health, education, jobs, joy and happiness, guests, and importantly wealth.

GREATER LONDON AUTHORITY

Today, Tamils all around the world, as a part of their house-warming practice, ensure that the milk is 'boiled' first and let that overflow and share that milk (by removing it from the cooker immediately, once it starts overflowing) to ensure that the house will be abundantly blessed and prosperous for the years to come.

Jallikattu is an ancient sport with a history spanning over 3,000 years and is part of the Pongal celebration. It is similar to Spanish bullfighting, which began in the 8th century AD, but with a key difference: Jallikattu does not involve killing the bull, and participants are not allowed to use weapons. The objective of Jallikattu is to tame and control the bulls. Jallikattu is one of the world's oldest sports still practiced today.

We have gone through all important parts of Tamil heritage, history and culture. In the next chapter, we shall get to the kitchen, but also discover some more details of the ancient, authentic, and original Tamil curry of pre-chilli and post-chilli eras.

FAMOUS TAMILS

- Tharman Sanmugaratnam, President of Singapore, is a Tamil
- Sundar Pichai, Google CEO, is a Tamil
- Indira Nooyi, recent CEO of Pepsi co, is a Tamil
- V. A. Shiva Ayyadurai, credited as the inventor of email, is a Tamil,.
- Mathematician and Father of Library Science, S.R. Ranganathan, was a Tamil.
- The winner of the 1930 Nobel Prize in Physics, C V Raman was a Tamil.
- Venkatraman Ramakrishnan- Nobel prize winner in 2009 , for studies and structure of ribosomes
- Abdul Kalam, a scientist who played a leading role in the development of India's missile and nuclear weapons programs and later became President of India, was a Tamil
- A R Rahaman, Oscar Music Winner for 'Slumdog Millionaire' was a Tamil!

CHAPTER 10

Bringing back ancient beverages and revealing some secret recipes.

Time to Get Cooking!

Yes, now, let's get cooking! Here are some of my favourite recipes as well as ideas for preparing Tamil dishes. Let's start our recipe list off with congee (also called Kanji or Konji). The name is derived from Tamil, where it was once a staple dish and is still widely consumed today. Also according to the Oxford English Dictionary, the English version may have entered the language via Portuguese in the 16th century, in a similar way that the word 'curry' did. Today, it is also used in other south Indian languages that split off from Tamil long ago. All this underlines just how old this dish is.

Congee is traditionally a by-product of rice cooking. Rice is boiled in more water than is necessary, and when the rice is properly cooked, the extra water is drained out. This thick water, which is rich in bran and vitamins, is then salted and often given to the household while it waits for the proper meal, rice with curries, to be prepared. This congee is sometimes used to feed domesticated cattle. Sometime leftover rice of the previous day, mixed with yogurt, onion, one or two green chillies, salt and lime pickle is also called Congee too. To differentiate this is referred as old congee because of the usage of old rice.

There are numerous old Tamil poems, songs, and tales about the women who brought this congee to the men who toiled in the paddy fields or on farms. The songs these women sang along the way were widely documented. The farmers, who were primarily peasants, would not eat heavy food, such as rice and curry, while they were working. Instead, they would prefer light food, like as congee, and then in the afternoon, after finishing their labour, they would eat heavy food, such as rice and curry. A by-product of cooking rice, congee, consequently gained popularity.

On the other hand, congee, which is just rice cooked with additional water, salt, and occasionally split green gram and coconut milk, can be made as a stand-alone porridge dish. This dish continues to be served to individuals in temporary shelters after a natural catastrophe or for any other reason in Southern India or Sri Lanka. After all, congee is simple and quick to prepare. When there isn't enough rice for everyone to have a full serving, additional people can be served at least one cup by adding extra water and making the congee a little runnier.

There are numerous variations from the basic congee

made with rice. The list includes millet congee (there are various types of millets available), mung (dhal – green gram) congee, urid (dhal black gram) congee, and much more.

Moreover, if the main ingredient is ground into flour and then used instead, the term "congee" transforms into "khali" (pudding) or "Koolz" (thick batter) when additional ingredients are incorporated.

Canja de galinha is the name of a popular chicken and rice soup in Portugal. The dish must have been brought by the Portuguese from their Tamil colony in the northern part of Sri Lanka. Millet-based congee is also particularly well-liked in Tamil-speaking regions. These simple vegan congees can be tweaked to become non-vegetarian congees. We'll examine this type in more detail in the recipe section.

In countries where the cooking of curry is widespread, congee is popular too. China, Japan, Taiwan, Korea, Thailand, Cambodia, Laos, Vietnam, Indonesia, and Malaysia all have congees as part of their food culture.

I'd also like to mention a robust snack known as "odiyal." It is derived from the tubers of the palmyra palm, specifically Palmyra sprouts. The process usually involves splitting these tubers lengthwise and allowing them to dry in the sun until they harden. Once they've reached the desired hardness, they are pounded to create a flour known as "Odiyal Flour.

Pulukodiyal is made by boiling and subsequently drying the tubers, a process that yields Pulukodiyal flour.

Odiyal serves as a primary ingredient in various food products, including **Odiyal flour, Odiyal chips, Odiyal pittu, Odiyal khool, Palm posha,** and more. It is a beloved snack among the Tamil communities in both of its natural habitats.

Since Tamil regions had many of palmyra trees, it is

likely that the Portuguese were the ones who thought of utilising odiyal flour as a thickener in the 16th century.

The abundant seafood found around the islets, including fish, crab, squid, and prawns, is combined with vegetables such as manioc, jackfruit seeds, beans, and moringa leaves (drumstick tree leaves), among others, to create a dish known as Odiyal khool. Odiyal flour is utilized as a thickening agent.

Whenever they felt a little under the weather with a cold or a cough,, Tamil grandfathers and grandmothers would prefer a trip to the market over a visit to the doctor or pharmacy. They would gather the necessary ingredients to prepare and enjoy a spicy Khool, which was their remedy for these minor discomforts!

The spiciness of Khool, can be quite intense, and it's amusing to witness people consuming it while their eyes and nostrils water. In fact, it doesn't have to be extremely hot to evoke this reaction. When a non-Tamil guest is invited to a Tamil home and served this treat, it's a clear indication of how much they value and respect the visitor. We'll delve into this recipe later on as well.

The Portuguese-era dish **"Odiyal khool"** is a special seafood soup that is only found in the Jaffna peninsula after initially appearing on the Islets. It is undoubtedly a delicacy from the post-chilli era and often the spiciness achieved through red chili, that have been ground into a paste.

Mulligatawny, which we've already talked a lot about, is often sold in small packets as powder or as liquid in cans, under different brand names. This is a far cry from the original version. This dish's traditional Tamil recipe will be provided later.

Neecha-tawny, is another food worth a quick mention as these days a bio drink company is offering this in tiny bottles and charging a premium price as it gains popularity in the

USA. Also at a premium price, it is also sold in bottles in Japan and in UAE.

You are probably aware that yoghurt is healthy since it is made from milk after it has been allowed to ferment by beneficial bacteria. Well, Tamils learned long ago that the same health advantages could be obtained from leftover rice if it was allowed to ferment with water and then taken the following day. The name Neechatawny refers to this fermented rice with water.

However, adding diluted yoghurt (buttermilk) will increase the benefit by twofold because both are fermented. Additionally, if onions, salt, one or two green chillies, and some lime pickles are added; the taste is wonderful.

This is a popular breakfast choice for the Tamil peasants mentioned before. You should definitely think about drinking Neechatawny often for health reasons. There isn't much you need to do for this healthy drink.

Instead of throwing leftover rice out, place it in a container with enough water to completely cover it, and then leave it outside or even in the refrigerator. Simply use it the following day with yogurt and other ingredients. Compared to other breakfast items, it is far healthier.

It has lately regained popularity in Tamil areas, and several restaurants are now serving it as a morning dish because of the high demand as many people switch back to these traditional drinks from the western drinks such as Coke and Pepsi.

Wekkaith Tawny or Moortawny

There is an ancient adage in the Tamil language: "Pankuni Maathathu Pakal Poluthil Veethiyali Popavanaip Paarthirupavan Paavi".

Ravi Maniam

பங்குனி மாதத்து பகல் பொழுதில், வீதி வழி
போபவனைப் பார்த்திருப்பவன் பாவி

"Those who merely watch someone walking along the street in the scorching midday sun of the month of Panguni are committing a great sin.."

"This phrase implies that individuals who are at ease, observing someone walking under the scorching sun during the month of Panguni, should extend the gesture of offering refreshments and inviting the person to rest until the sun's intensity and temperature subside. Failing to do so might be viewed as an act lacking in ethics or humanity..."

*Panguni - is a Tamil Month, (March/April) when the sun is directly above and the midday temperature is typically very high.

Wekkai(th) Tawny or Moor(th) Tawny is a Buttermilk Drink used to relieve thirst in a humid environment (the Tamil word 'Wekkai' refers to humidity). Regardless of the religion they practise, some volunteers put up pandals (marques) at the sides of the road in Tamil areas to distribute drinks like these to pilgrims who make lengthy journeys in the hot sun to their places of worship during festive sessions.

Pilgrims, instead of using vehicles, often take vows to walk many miles to worship. They would normally be offered Wekkai Tanne(r) along their way.

This is basically a drink of buttermilk (diluted yoghurt mixed with onion, salt, one or two chillies, and some lime pickle in the right measurements). It is one of the best and healthiest old beverages. If you taste it, I guarantee you'll prefer this to a cold beer.

Keep in mind that yoghurt drinks are typically considered sweet desserts in the West

The Sambal

The Sambal is the precursor of Peri-Peri (Piri-Piri) sauce. Peri-Peri sauce is said to be originated from Mozambique, a colony of Portugal. It is used as a spice or marinade and is particularly popular in Angola, Namibia, Mozambique, and South Africa. It is not been clarified where the Portuguese got the idea from.

In reality, the Dutch deserve more credit for the Peri-Peri (Piri-Piri) innovation than the Portuguese, as Sambal served as its forerunner. Today, Sambal continues to be quite popular in Sri Lanka, Malaysia, and Indonesia, all of which were once Dutch and Portuguese colonies. The Dutch introduced the practice of adding alcohol to food in the island nation of Ceylon. Another post-chilli era innovation that the Dutch introduced was the use of vinegar in food, as well as marinating a well-known rich cake with fruits in brandy. However, the addition of vinegar to Peri-Peri distinguishes it from Sambal. Additionally, Peri-Peri sauce is simmered, unlike Sambal.

When we delve into the ingredients of traditional pre-chilli Sambal, we discover black peppers, onions, salt, and lime. The Portuguese introduced and popularised chillies, leading to further evolution in sambal. This evolution involved replacing black peppers with chillies or making chillies the primary ingredient (with fewer or no black peppers).

Consequently, the predecessor of Peri-Peri Sauce can be traced back to the Tamil Sambal, which was further developed by substituting pepper with the chillies introduced by the Portuguese to the Tamil region. The newly developed innovative curry powder was then introduced in the Portuguese African colonies (notably 'berbere' in Ethiopia) and also to far-eastern colonies and trading nations, including Thailand, China, and Japan.

Indeed, this culinary journey is intricate and captivating. It all begins with Tamil Sambal in Portuguese Ceylon, extends through different Portuguese colonies in Africa, and ultimately contributes to the evolution of Peri-Peri Sauce. Notably, South Africa was a Dutch colony simultaneously with Ceylon, Malacca, and Indonesia. This Dutch colonial connection is an intriguing aspect of the culinary history associated with Nando's expansion.

The Sambal - Varieties

Let me say a bit more about how to make the Sambal. The basic ingredients for many years have been the same: black pepper, onion, salt, and either lime or tamarind.

With the introduction of chillies by the Portuguese, black pepper was replaced by the chillies. Or it becomes 'Coconut Sambal', when grated coconut is added.

There are many varieties of popular Sambals:

- Pounded Sambal
- Ground Sambal (Red or Green)
- Simple Sambal with curry powder
- Dried Fish Sambal
- Dried Tuna Fish Sambal
- Prawn Sambal
- Aubergine Sambal
- Ginger Sambal
- Vallarai Leaf (Asiatic pennywort) Sambal
- Seeni Sambal (Caramalised Onion Sambal)

Here are a few of my favourites as well as how to make them.

Coconut Sambal

Coconut Sambal (Theng-kaai Sambal) is made of scraped coconut (thengkaai mean coconut in Tamil, - remember, 'kaai'), onion, green chilli, red chilli powder, and lime juice as its main ingredients. Sometimes, crumbled dried Tuna fish is also added, and tomatoes can be used instead of lime juice for flavor.

Salty Chilli Sambal

This is a paste of red chilli pounded with sea salt. A widespread derivative is Katta sambal, which adds onions, crumbled dried Tuna fish, salt, and lime juice to the chilli-and-salt mixture. This goes very well with coconut milk rice dish.

Vaalai kaai (Raw Curry Banana) sambal

This is another sambal made of boiled and mashed plantain, scraped coconut, chopped green chillies and onion, salt, and lime juice. Vaalai kaai means unripe plantain in Tamil.

Seeni Sambal (Caramalised Onion Sambal)

This recipe includes onion, crumbled dried tuna fish (we discussed this already), and spices as its main ingredients. We will see this in detail later, once you taste this delicacy, you will only feel how come you never knew about this before.

Cooking Methods

Let us move on to another important topic now: the cooking methods for curries. We all know that there are numerous ways to cook food. Today, microwave ovens can also be used for cooking but there are also many more traditional methods.

Roasting

The discovery of the very first cooking method was likely accidental, as early humans, like other animals, initially consumed hunted animal flesh raw. Over time, hunters might have encountered animals that had been cooked by natural wildfires. This led them to realize that roasting the hunted animal made it tastier and more tender than consuming it raw.

In modern cooking, techniques such as grilling, roasting in an oven, and cooking over an open flame have evolved. When it comes to curry, marinating the dish with 'Curry Thuool' before roasting is often superior to using sauces or curry pastes.

Steaming

Steaming is a prevalent cooking method for various popular dishes, including Idly, String Hoppers, Pittu, different types of rice, and some snacks. Tamils, like other prominent civilizations, often lived close to riverbanks.

In the absence of tools for digging wells to access fresh and filtered water, living near rivers provided them with a reliable source for cultivating essential crops and cooking. However, they soon realized that frequently flooded river water wasn't always safe for cooking.

Consequently, ancient Tamils turned to steam cooking, which they found to be a much healthier alternative. While not as common in the West, steam cooking remains a popular practice among Tamils.

Sautéing

The introduction of this French culinary style to the island is credited to the Portuguese. The Tamils of the Indian subcontinent, not having been influenced by the Portuguese, were initially unfamiliar with this practice. However, they began to catch up with it during the British colonial era.

In the Tamil language, there are two words to describe frying. "Poriyal" refers to deep frying, while "Waruval" denotes a method that uses little to no oil. The word "Warai" likely originated from "Waruval."

A particularly well-liked cuisine among the Tamils of the Island is the sautéing of certain vegetables or leaves, known generally as Warai. To name a few of these common Warai foods, there is cabbage warai, muringa leaves warai, greens (leaves) warai, crab warai, and baby sharks (fish) warai. This technique can also be used to prepare some meat.

Additionally, popular South Indian dishes like Dosa, Hopper, and street foods such as Kothu Roti, Pocket Roti, Coconut Roti, and Curry Stuffed Roti can be considered extensions of the technique of cooking on a griddle or skillet with minimal to no oil.

Roti-Paratha

The dish known popularly as Roti in Sri Lanka, refers to bread in Southern India and so it is known as Paratha there. It should not be confused with Naan or Chapati of (North) India. Bread is not a common breakfast option in India, in contrast to the island of Sri Lanka.

This might be due to the island having been occupied by Europeans for 450 years as opposed to 150 years in India.

According to an Australian chef, the name Bread-Roti was changed to Parotta (Paratha) in India. Later, we'll see a variety of Rotis, including Koththu Roti (Chopped Roti), a highly famous street food among Tamils and a favourite of young people on the island, in Tamil Nadu, and elsewhere who go out on Friday nights or the weekends. 'Koththu Paratha' is a term used in Tamil Nadu for what is known in Sri Lanka as 'Koththu Roti'. Both refer to the same brilliant delicacy. Roti is popular in Malaysia, and in Singapore, its government has taken steps to promote it to tourists.

Baking

The Portuguese can be credited with introducing a baking tradition to the island of Sri Lanka and possibly South East Asia. They played a significant role in popularising the use of wheat flour, leading to the development of cake, bread, biscuits, and the cultivation of at least one hundred and thirty other fruits, chillies, vegetables, and plants.

The Tamil people on the island began incorporating wheat flour into their diet alongside rice, rice flour, and various types of millet flour they had traditionally used. With the emergence of coffee booths, cafes, and the introduction of cakes and various quick meals made from wheat flour, it became a staple food in this early Portuguese colony in Asia. Wheat flour was used to make bread, buns, and roti.

It's interesting to note that among the Tamils, it seems that only those from the Jaffna peninsula practice steaming wheat flour to eliminate its stickiness before using it to prepare dishes such as pittu and string hoppers, which are traditionally made with rice flour. This practice is so common that steamed wheat flour is now readily available in packets in Tamil retail stores in the West, similar to plain flour.

The use of both plain and steamed wheat flour has given rise to a variety of snacks commonly known as short eats. We will explore many of these snacks in the recipe sections. I would suggest recommending these snacks to coffee houses,

Curry heritage of the Tamils

as many of the options available today are either loaded with cheese or sugar, which could potentially become targets for government health initiatives in the future.

Smoking

The Dutch introduced the practice of smoking tobacco leaves to preserve and transport them to distant markets, which led to the establishment of a small cottage industry in Tamil Nadu for rolling and exporting cigars.

Today, Tamils use smoking as a method to expedite the ripening of certain fruits, such as bananas and mangoes (the process of making "Kaai to Pazham"). However, using smoking as a preservation method is not common among Tamils, possibly due to the abundant sunlight available.

Frying

The Tamil people have been using this technique for a long time. Initially, they likely used cow ghee (butter) for frying before transitioning to other vegetable oils. Frying is a common method for preparing various celebratory snacks, including Vadai (made from both Urid dal and Chana dal), Curry Rolls, Stuffed Roti, and numerous traditional snacks such as mixers, murukku, and green gram pie, commonly known as 'Short Eats.'

This method is employed to create delicious and popular dishes like 'Fish Fry,' 'Prawn Fry,' 'Squid Fry,' and others. The key to imparting these dishes with their heavenly flavor is by coating or mixing them with Tamil Curry Thuool (Curry Powder).

The curried fried egg or curried omelette is another noteworthy dish worth mentioning in this context. It serves as an ideal accompaniment to rice, string hoppers, pittu, roti, or even as a filling for a sandwich with bread. This delicious curried omelette originated when Portuguese colonialists introduced the dish 'Spanish omelette,' and Tamils added their characteristic curry thuool twist to it.

Typically, however, the Tamils do not prepare their staple foods by frying.

Boiling

Rice is most commonly cooked by boiling, which is the prevalent method. Additionally, boiling is a key method in various curry preparations, as nearly all curry ingredients are typically boiled, either alone or with other components, before being combined to create a final curry dish.

Some ingredients for curries are fried first, then boiled with other ingredients. Later, we'll see a lot more.

Drying

I refer to this as a "secondary method" of preparing ingredients because dried foods typically require rehydration by boiling or frying. The preservation technique known as drying involves removing moisture from the food, thereby inhibiting bacterial growth.

Food preservation methods with ancient origins include open-air drying using the sun and wind. This practice predates the widespread use of refrigeration. In regions with cold climates, such as Scotland, the traditional smoking of fish has become a longstanding tradition.

In Tamil areas, where abundant sunlight is available, people prefer drying food rather than smoking it. This method involves salting, drying, and preserving excess meat and seafood for future use.

Indeed, sultanas, raisins, tomotos and other similar items are sun-dried, much like the process used to dry ripe red chili fruits into dried red chilies. Tamil vegetarians often integrate dried ingredients into their "saiva" curry meals, including items like buttermilk chilli (green chillies marinated in diluted salty yogurt and then dried), "vadakam" (dried items made from neem tree flowers), and the familiar poppadoms. Additionally, some exceptional and delectable curry dishes, mostly undiscovered by Western tastes, feature dried meats, dried fish, dried prawns, and various other dried ingredients.

The curries that will truly tantalize your taste buds include those featuring potatoes and dried fish, curry with eggplants and dried fish, and a mildly-spiced white curry with dried prawns. You won't be able to resist wanting more. I promise!

Dried tuna fish flakes are a hidden gem among curry ingredients, capable of imparting a unique flavor to any vegetable curry and even transforming it into a non-vegetarian dish. Unlike other raw fish, tuna is first boiled and cooked, and then its flesh is dried in the sun before being crushed into flakes. You can add these flakes to the red-chili sambal I mentioned earlier.

So why not try making a dried fish fry? Your neighbours will surely come knocking, and they won't leave until they've savored some!

Pre-cooking and Post-cooking marination

With this method, typically the food is prepared with sauces and left to marinate before cooking. For example, chicken is marinated in sauces before cooking.

But what about marinating after cooking?

In essence, this means eating the post-cooked, marinated curry the next day. This is a delight you wouldn't want to miss.

Tamils often make slightly more food than is necessary for family gatherings like weddings and birthday parties because it is considered disrespectful to have not prepared enough food for the invited guests, with 'not enough' being shown by having no leftovers.

In many traditional Tamil families, it's a common practice for Granny to gather the leftover rice and curries in a large vessel the day after a gathering. She mixes these leftovers and later shares them with other family members. This communal meal is typically rolled into a big circle and served on leaves, carried in the palm, and eaten in mouthfuls. While various leaves can be used, many prefer a particular type, such as the portia tree leaf.

Nobody wants to miss out on this treat! As you enjoy it with your entire family and all of the relatives who came together to celebrate the previous day, it is the memorable event of love and joy. Later in the recipe section, we will see this in more detail. By the way, personally, I prefer my rice, pittu, or roti with post-cook marinated seafood curries like crab, fish, or prawn.

The White Curry

We've already discussed white curry. In general, Europeans, notably the Portuguese, encouraged Tamils to use coconut milk to reduce the spiciness of chili after discovering that chili was spicier than black pepper. As chili naturally turned curries red, other curries that began to emerge without any chili became known as white curries (as coconut milk makes them white). It's important to note that the Portuguese introduced many new vegetables, leading to various fresh culinary approaches. This period can be aptly referred to as the "Curry Renaissance."

Today, among the Tamils, very few curries are made without coconut milk, signifying a culinary style quite distinct from the heavily modified pre-chili era curries commonly served in the West, which are gradually losing popularity. It's worth noting that even in contemporary Asian cuisines like Thai Green and Red Curries and Japanese Katsu Curry, coconut milk and chili powder are used, underscoring the enduring cultural connections between Portuguese and Tamil culinary influences, even after the advent of the chilli.

In the UK's "Indian Curry Houses," where coconut milk was not traditionally common in pre-chili era curries, sugar is often used as a substitute to reduce the spiciness in curry paste. "Double Cream" is another common replacement, as seen in dishes like "Chicken Tikka Masala Curry." Unfortunately, these substitutions have led to well-known complaints about the unhealthiness of some curry dishes.

Last but not least: 'Thalitham' (தாளிதம்)

This unique method of garnishing, tempering, or seasoning is a secret technique to enhance the flavors of the curry. It is not widely known outside Tamil culture, and there isn't a meaningful English word for it, so the Tamil term is used instead.

The difference between Thalitham and other types of seasonings used in Tamil cooking is the addition of fried spices and other ingredients to curries either before or after they have finished cooking to enhance their flavour.

This technique is vital for many Tamils, especially vegetarians. When we examine the recipes later, we'll see this.

Curry: Various Options

In the West, it's common to see a plate with one half filled with rice and the other half with a curry, often of the chicken variety. While it's a common way of serving curry in the West, it may not provide the full and authentic curry experience.

A combination of curries prepared using various techniques not only creates the perfect curry meal but also offers variety. Without this variety, a dinner consisting solely of items like rice and chicken curry, which are both cooked by boiling, can become unappealing and monotonous.

Indeed, a meal that includes Red Raw Rice (steamed), Chicken Curry (boiled), Beans Curry (shallow fried), Cabbage Warai (sauteed), an onion and carrot salad, and fried poppadum offers a diverse and intriguing range of flavors and textures, providing a more exciting and varied dining experience.

In Tamil areas, the tradition of eating poppadum with Saiva or Vegetarian meals continues, and it's not typically served with non-vegetarian meals, in contrast to practices in the UK or in the West. Cultural dining traditions often offer unique insights into the local culinary customs.

The next topic that I want to discuss is what I call 'taste-ology', By this, I mean to start a conversation about taste. This is crucial because it allows us to understand how the various tastes interact to create the overall curry experience.

CHAPTER 11

Considering Different Types of Tastes and Combinations.

Did you know that the human tongue is capable of sensing six different types of tastes - அறுசுவைகள்? Amazingly, this fact appears in ancient Tamil literature. This is how they are put together.

- ✓ Taste 1: Sweet - இனிப்பு – inippu eg: sugarcane or palm sugar
- ✓ Taste 2: Bitter - கசப்பு – kasappu eg: bitter gourd,

✓ Taste 3: Astringent - துவர்ப்பு – Tuvarppu eg: Unripe or raw Banana or Pomegranate, chickpeas, green beans, okra, cranberries

✓ Taste 4: Sour - புளிப்பு - puLippu eg: Tamarind, Lime, Vinegar, Sour Mango, Sour Tomato, Yoghurt

✓ Taste 5: Salty - உவர்ப்பு - uvarppu eg: Sea Salt

✓ Taste 6: Spicy or Pungent – கார்ப்பு /உறைப்பு - Kaarppu/ Uraippu eg. Chilli, Black Pepper, Paprika

Undoubtedly, the popularity of curry hinges on its remarkable capacity to harmonize and balance a diverse array of flavors, culminating in a delightful and satisfying culinary experience.

The art of achieving this equilibrium and determining the perfect proportions is a skill unto itself. If you're eager to delve into the intricacies of flavor components, their interactions, or perhaps explore the distinctive flavor profiles of specific curry types, I invite you to visit my website for more details at thatscurry.com

The Tastes

The essence of a curry lies in skillfully combining ingredients with diverse tastes in precise proportions to harmonize with the flavor of the main ingredient, often dominant, resulting in a truly delightful culinary experience.

Take, for example, bitter gourd, a natural remedy advocated by organizations like Diabetic UK. On its own, it can be a challenging taste for many to consume. However, by skillfully combining it with other flavors – salty, sweet, spicy, or sour – in precise proportions, it can be transformed into a delectable bitter gourd curry dish.

Indeed, sambal is a remarkable culinary creation and a precursor to various sauces like chili sauce, ketchup, and peri-

Curry heritage of the Tamils

peri sauce. What makes it exceptional is the balance of at least four different tastes. Basic sambal incorporates the elements of hot and spicy (chili), bitter and sweet (onion), salty (sea salt), and sour (lime or tamarind) in perfect harmony.

As you see, curry is a skillful manipulation of taste that caters to our taste buds. A skilled chef understands how to create flavorful curries. Ingredients like aubergine (eggplant) or potatoes, which lack a distinct flavor themselves, are incredibly versatile and can be prepared in numerous ways, resulting in a wide variety of delicious dishes.

To enhance the flavor of meat, we often incorporate salt and various seasonings. Therefore, a curry is essentially the perfect blend of diverse flavors with the meat or seafood as its central component. A meat or seafood curry doesn't necessarily require a sweet taste, and when using pineapple in a curry, it's essential to balance its natural sourness.

In our discussion earlier about the ancient dish of the Tamils, 'Uhoon Soru',(meat rice) we saw that one of the ingredients was honey. The Arabs did not add this in their biriyani dish. Later, learning from experience, the Tamils too stopped adding honey to non-sweet foods. Actually, this is one reason why Tamils in the west don't use the so-called 'Curry Paste' from the supermarket – because it includes sugar in addition to other odd components like maize. The Tamils never use sugar in their freshly prepared curry paste or Curry Thuool (Curry Powder).

The flavor profiles for vegetable curries can vary widely. The best combinations of flavors for different vegetable curries will become apparent as we explore the recipe section. For instance, when preparing a tomato curry, there's often little to no need for lime or tamarind juice because tomatoes have a natural sweet and sour taste. On the other hand, when making a potato curry, which is more neutral in flavor, adding lime or tamarind juice is a common way to introduce a sour element.

Similarly, as meat and seafood are neutral in taste, they require the addition of flavours like sour, salt, spice, and onion to make it tasty. On the other hand, dry fish already contains salt, therefore a curry with it, doesn't need to be salted.

Furthermore, when working with a Chilli Curry (yep, a curry with chilli as the main ingredient!), known for its inherent spiciness due to the primary role of chillies, it's crucial to balance and mellow that spiciness. In accordance with the well-established Tamil culinary tradition, tamarind juice is frequently employed to enhance seafood dishes, as it harmonizes with their flavors. In contrast, meat-based dishes often incorporate lime juice to introduce an additional sour element.

It's consistently disheartening to observe that the curry paste available in supermarkets is primarily designed for non-vegetarian curries, such as chicken or occasionally mutton. This leaves customers with limited options when they desire to prepare dishes like vegetarian potato curry, fried aubergine sour curry, and various others. Since one universal curry paste cannot be adapted to suit the specific characteristics of each dish, the choices for vegetarians become even more limited.

Okay, I'm confident you now understand the concept. Now that we have covered the basic details but before we get into the recipe section, let's talk about some food traditions.

Food Traditions

The Tamil people have developed a diverse array of culinary traditions over thousands of years. One such tradition is the observance of a vegetarian day of the week.

According to family customs, one day each week is designated as a vegetarian day.

In their native Tamil Nadu and Sri Lanka, the majority of Tamils typically observe Friday as a day of complete vegetarianism. However, this day of observance may vary among the Tamil diaspora.

On this designated day, the lady of the household cleans the house and kitchen, using utensils, plates, cups, and cutlery exclusively for vegetarian (vegan) dishes, ensuring they are not mixed with those used for non-veg dishes. Only vegetarian or vegan food is prepared and served on this day.

This practice, especially for the well-being of children's health, is highly recommended to anyone. It's beneficial if this practice can be linked to the beliefs and values your family adheres to.

It's worth noting that Taiwan encourages weekly vegetarian meals. Israel has been hosting annual vegetarian festivals since 2014. Approximately 13% of the populations of Taiwan and Israel adhere to vegetarian or vegan diets. India stands out with the world's highest percentage of vegetarians, at 38%. In Europe, Italy leads with the largest proportion of vegetarians at 10%, followed by the UK, Germany, and Austria, each with 9%. In the Americas, Brazil is the sole nation with a substantial percentage of vegetarians, estimated at 8%.

Keep in mind that the well-being of a nation is significantly influenced by the practices in our household kitchens.

Cold and warm meats

For centuries, the Tamil people have recognized the qualities of different meats, categorizing chicken as a 'warm meat' and mutton as a 'cold meat.' They employ this knowledge to guide individuals in deciding whether to include or abstain from specific types of meat, taking into account their physical attributes and the prevailing weather conditions, such as cold, rainy, or warm conditions.

According to these customs, pregnant women and nursing mothers are advised to be cautious about their dietary choices. Nursing mothers are encouraged to include certain types of fish, such as small milk shark, in their diet to stimulate increased milk production for their infants.

The milk shark, Rhizoprionodon acutus, is a species of requiem shark and a member of the Carcharhinidae family. The Tamil people have the belief that eating milk shark meat encourages lactation.

These are always small and never more than one meter in length. The milk shark is widespread and resilient but nonetheless the International Union for Conservation of Nature has listed the milk shark as vulnerable.

Providing light and easily digestible meals is essential for infants, young children, the elderly, individuals recuperating from illnesses like the flu or cold, and patients in post-surgery recovery. Traditional wisdom suggests that while rice and curries may not be considered light foods, dishes made with rice flour are.

('Hopper' (Appam) and 'String Hopper' (Idi Appam) are the English names given by British officials who tasted these dishes. This is why I mentioned earlier that if the British had created 'Mulligatawny' soup, it might have been named 'Black Pepper Soup, instead.)

Another traditional Tamil food practice involves the use of herbs to cleanse the stomach and intestines. It's important to note that this is an outdated custom, and I do not recommend its revival. This information is provided for historical context.

In the past, Tamil grandmothers were often tasked with "cleaning the stomach and intestines," which essentially involved administering certain herbs with laxative effects. By encouraging repeated restroom visits on that day, the goal was to flush out undesirable substances from the body.

The household would then be treated to a feast the following day. While this practice may still exist in some isolated Tamil villages, it is no longer commonplace.

I should also discuss which curries complement each other well. For many Tamils, a meat curry, be it mutton or chicken, pairs excellently with aubergine white curry, beetroot white curry, cabbage warai, and rasam. However, dhal (red lentil) curry isn't the ideal accompaniment for a meat curry, even though it's a common practice in many curry restaurants. This is because both red lentils and meat are rich in protein, which doesn't create a well-balanced meal.

The Traditional Tamil Vegetarian Meal

On the cover of this book, you can observe a traditional Tamil curry meal presented on a banana leaf. Each of the six taste buds on the tongue is stimulated by various elements of the meal. However, it's important to note that a single curry served with rice and poppadom does not constitute a typical curry meal, despite the common misconception held by many non-Tamils.

These days, in Tamil areas and among Tamils, vegetarian meals are often referred to as, 'Saiva Meals'. I have no idea why and or how but referring to them this way is something that again comes from ancient times. The term 'Saivam' refers to a subsect of Hinduism. The majority of Tamil people are Saivas, or people who worship Lord Shiva as their primary deity.

Therefore, in regions inhabited by Tamils, you'll come

across "Saiva" (சைவ) restaurants, which essentially translate to "Pure Vegetarian" restaurants.

Tamils often use the expression "It's a Saiva day for me," signifying that they are abstaining from non-vegetarian foods for that particular day, even if they typically consume them. Another instance is, "Let's dine out for a Saiva meal."

Eating with fingers

I encountered a profound sentiment on the wall of a vegetarian eatery: "There are few pleasures greater than feeling dal and rice squish between your fingers." I wholeheartedly agree, as eating with my hands instead of a fork has enabled me to expertly blend food flavors without any interference from the metallic taste of cutlery. So, I'm in complete agreement!

There's an anecdote from an Indian newspaper about the occasion when a President of India visited 10 Downing Street and joined a dinner hosted by Winston Churchill. During the meal, the president began eating with his fingers, and Churchill, famous for his candidness, remarked, "Mr. President, please don't take offense, but I believe using a spoon or fork is much healthier."

The president, a vegetarian, responded with a smile, "But Prime Minister, at least I'm certain that my fingers haven't been in other people's mouths."

Mr. Churchill chuckled, unable to refute the point.

This little story brings me to the topic of what makes a traditional curry kitchen and what you will need in your cupboard for an authentic 'Tamil' curry meal.

Curry heritage of the Tamils

Here's my list of essentials.

Fenugreek	Mustard	Cloves
Cumin seeds	Green and Red Chillies	Curry Leaves
Fennel seeds	Cardamom	Bay leaves
Black Pepper	Star annas	Panden Leaves
Garlic	Turmeric	Coriander leaves
Ginger	Coriander	Asafoetida (optional)
Onions	Cinnamon	**Roasted Curry Powder**

Roasted Curry Powder (Tamil-Portuguese)

As previously mentioned, Tamils don't utilise store-bought 'Curry Paste,' which, as you now understand, is a pre-chilli era blend but altered to deviate from the original that Tamils create and use. Instead, they rely on specially crafted 'Roasted Curry Thuool' (Curry Powder). The concept behind this is that all the essential spices are present in the correct proportions, as it was a fusion of Portuguese and Tamil culinary traditions nearly five hundred years ago.

When working with what is commonly referred to as 'Indian Curry' recipes, Westerners can frequently become perplexed by instructions like a spoon of this spice, half a spoon of that spice, and another spoon of something else, and so forth.

Nevertheless, with Tamil's roasted "Curry Thuool" (Curry Powder), all the ingredients are already harmoniously proportioned, eliminating such sources of frustration. You only need to add one or two spoons, adjusting according to your desired level of spiciness.

The main food items with which the curries will be eaten are:
- ✓ Rice
- ✓ Items made out of rice flour, gram flour, and wheat flour: String hoppers, Hoppers, Pittu, Roti, Idly, Dosa.
- ✓ Items made with various millets flour.
- ✓ Other items that can be eaten with curry: Bread, Throw Roti, Layered Roti, Paratha, Chapati and Naan.

Hence, I hope you agree that curry or curries are not the main food but they are accompanying dishes for the main food.

"By the way, have you ever tasted tin sandwich bread with freshly prepared curry, such as prawn curry or potato curry, especially if you follow a vegetarian or vegan diet?"

Different varieties of Rice

In English, there is only one word: Rice, whether it is uncooked or cooked. But in Tamil, there are three separate words. Rice is called 'arisi' for uncooked and 'Soru' for cooked rice and 'Pazhaya Soru' for one-day-old cooked rice. (pazhaya means old and old soru).

There are so many different varieties of rice. Thousands of them! 22,000 to give a rough idea. Yet in the West, we are familiar with Basmati rice and long-grain rice. Many Western cooks prefer using long-grain rice to avoid the issue of rice turning "mushy" or "pulpy." (I will give a bit more of an explanation later.)

Let's begin with Basmati rice, which is a product originating from Northern India and Pakistan. On the other hand, Jasmine rice hails from Thailand. Interestingly, Basmati rice hasn't been widely popular among Tamils yet. Instead, Tamils have traditionally favored rice that is rich in bran, a preference that persists today.

Take the original rice, once de-husked. Unpolished rice is fully covered with bran. Some like it, many won't because it won't mix well with curries. Semi polished is known as, red-raw rice. This is what people use for Pongal, Congee and additionally red-raw rice pounded to make flour so that other items can be made. Basmati is fully polished white rice and so full of carbs.

Another process is to boil the paddy and then dry it in sunlight and then remove the husk. This way, the fibre and Vitamin B-rich bran are retained fully with the grain. Rice still with its bran is known as brown rice – or parboiled rice, a term which refers to the process of how it is made. People who love brown bread or brown cereal should love brown rice too. Diabetics should also opt for this. There are many different varieties to choose from, like Samba rice. This is very popular for its aromatic flavour and especially for Biryanis.

Black Rice or Forbidden Rice

It is called 'forbidden' because it was originally only the king or the royal family were consuming it, with the public forbidden to cultivate, harvest, or eat it. Black (Karupu) rice (arisi), also popularly known as black kavuni rice, lowers the risk of type 2 Diabetes.

Black Kavuni rice also contains the Important Antioxidant Vitamin E, which helps to maintain skin, eyes, and immune health. Karuppu Kavuni (hand pound black rice) also known as Emperor Rice. Kavuni Black rice helps to prevent cancer.

But the 'forbidden' was a thing of the past. You can enjoy it now. Although you may not like the taste. As we all are aware, healthy food are not necessarily tasty.

An explanation on mushy or pulpy rice (Cooked)

When you add more water than needed and forget to drain it (congee), the rice will continue to cook even after it is fully cooked, resulting in mushy or pulpy or sticky rice. Although some individuals enjoy it, it typically doesn't mix well with curries. Water measurement is crucial for this reason. Although many people use long-grain rice since it doesn't turn mushy, it is not at all tasty or mix well with curries, unlike basmati rice.

International Year of Millets - 2023

Small grains with a rounded shape are referred to as millet. Examples include finger millet, barnyard millet, foxtail millet, pearl millet, little millet, kodo millet, and sorghum millet.

Small grains were a significant part of the Tamil people's diet in the past, according to a variety of Sangam-era literary sources. According to Thirukkural, which we covered in a previous chapter, millet has been used in place of rice in a variety of dishes.

There is historical evidence suggesting that some of these millets were cultivated and consumed in the Indus Valley Civilization. The relationship between millets and Tamils has deep roots, and today, health-conscious individuals are turning to these grains as part of their efforts to maintain good health.

In the recipe sections, we'll explore various dishes, including congee, biriyani, and more, all featuring millets. Millets have made a significant comeback in Tamil kitchens and dining tables, and we'll also provide numerous recipes, which might be particularly appealing to dieters.

At its 75th session in March 2021, the United Nations

General Assembly proclaimed 2023 the International Year of Millets (IYM). The IYM 2023 provided an opportunity to increase public awareness of millets' health and nutritional advantages as well as their suitability for growing in challenging and changing climatic conditions.

It was an opportunity to 'highlight millets' ability to provide sustainable market prospects for producers and consumers while also promoting their sustainable development.

Chapter 12

Making the Authentic Tamil Curry.

The Tamil language has a proverb that reads, 'Food is medicine and medicine is food', reminding us that the Tamil people have a great deal of experience with nutrition. And of all the foods, curry is particularly passionately prepared.

There is a specific curry for bringing forth a baby who was past due, and there is another kind to encourage the nursing mother to produce more milk. Even minor infant illnesses can be healed by just switching the feeding mother's own diet. Light meals for those recovering from surgery and different meals for women going through menopause or young girls who have come to age.

Tamil philosophers, referred to as Siddhars, have a long and illustrious history that closely parallels the development of the Tamil language. These Siddhars were individuals who attained intellectual powers known as "siddhi," signifying enlightenment. In total, there were eighteen Siddhars in this tradition.

Agathiyar, the first Siddhar

The Siddhars acquired their knowledge through profound concentration, divine insights, and unwavering dedication to specific areas of study. They delved into diverse fields such as astrology, physics, technology, astronomy, literature, fine arts, music, drama, and dance. This extensive knowledge allowed them to offer assistance to the general population by providing remedies for ailments and offering guidance on future matters.

The Siddhars were multifaceted individuals, embodying roles as saints, physicians, alchemists, and mystics, all within a single persona. They documented their observations in the form of Tamil poems on palm leaves, and these were compiled and safeguarded as "Palm leaf manuscripts." Some families in Tamil regions still hold these manuscripts, passing them down through generations, while others are archived in public institutions like universities in countries such as India, Germany, the United Kingdom, and the United States.

Siddhars were celebrated for their extended, deep meditation practices, through which they attained enlightenment. Utilizing their meditative prowess, they identified and suggested certain plants and medicinal leaves for dietary consumption to alleviate specific ailments. Thanks to their guidance, at least forty-two diverse types of spinach and leaves are still used in curries. Furthermore, the flowers, stems, and tubers of banana trees are integrated into curries, holding medicinal properties for addressing various health issues.

The Philosophy of Curry

Curry is frequently mistaken as a dish. For the Tamil people, however, it is the centrepiece of the dish. For instance, if the dish is made with chicken, it is called chicken curry gravy (Kuzhambu), and if the dish is made with tomato, it is called tomato curry gravy or tomato Kuzhambu, in Tamil.

There are many types of curries.

1. Among the Tamil community, the term "Curry" is commonly referred to as "Kuzhambu," indicating a thin or runny curry.
2. Dry curry (not runny or a gravy) is known in Tamil as Piraddal.
3. Sauteed curry (fried with less or no oil/fat) is known in Tamil as Warai.
4. When fried, the curry is known in Tamil as Poriyal (Deep Fry) or Waruval.

All kinds of curry can be complemented with poppadum, sambal, chutney, and pickles (such as Lime, Mango, Fish or Prawn Pickles).

These curries can all be divided into two further categories: spicy and non-spicy. The non-spicy curry is often referred to as 'white curry' or 'milk curry' in Tamil (white or milk refers to less or no spiciness). This is primarily due to the Europeanisation of curry with the Tamils on the island of Ceylon.

Curry heritage of the Tamils

With the introduction of White Curry (Milk Curry) to Britain and the Western culinary scene, it's possible that more individuals who have avoided curry due to its perceived spiciness might reconsider. **This book aims to contribute to the broader awareness and adoption of white curries in Britain.**

Potato Kuzhambu curry is typically considered to be on the watery side. In contrast, when a dish lacks gravy and is relatively dry, it's referred to as "Pirattal" (dry curry). An example of this is Potato Pirattal.

Now, there's the Onion (or vendhaya curry) Kuzhambu curry. It's noteworthy that onion alone can make a delightful curry. A curry made solely with onions can be incredibly delicious, particularly appreciated by vegans. Given the option between Vendhaya Kuzhambu curry and Chicken Kuzhambu curry, I would choose the former. You'll likely agree once you've had a taste. Additionally, there's the exceptionally healthy Garlic Kuzhambu curry. (Vendhaya in Tamil means fenugreek*)

My grandmother couldn't explain why onion curry is sometimes called fenugreek (vendhaya) curry. Fenugreek is simply another spice, and it's not added to all curries, unlike onions. Avoiding confusion might be the reason behind this naming.

You may not have heard about vegetables like drumstick (Moringa), Snake gourd, Elephant foot yam, Long beans or Bread fruit curries. Sometime Tamils make curries with two or more vegetables together. Moringa and Potato curry, Beans and Potato fried curry, Long-beans and Jack fruit's seed curry, Pumpkin and Cassava curry, Mushroom and Potato curry are to name but a few.

It is possible to improve the taste of vegetable curries by

adding dried tuna fish flakes (thereby making it non-vegetarian).

Oh, I must not forget to tell you about a white curry with aubergine (Eggplant), and ash banana. However, it is impossible to list every variation of what I would call the true "Plant Based Diet" here.

Nonetheless, I hope that by now you are really beginning to get something of the idea of what an authentic curry is.

There are many different varieties of sambals. The traditional Tamil 'Fried and Pounded' chilli and coconut sambal goes very well with Tin sandwich bread. We will see some of these recipes later.

On Saturday mornings, I enjoy having fresh tin bread with coconut sambal and a cup of plain tea for breakfast.

Food parcel

Typically, on supermarket shelves, you can find ready-to-eat packs containing a portion of white rice and a portion of chicken curry (Example: Rice with Chicken Tikka Masala or Rice with Korma). These packs are designed for take-away, allowing you to take them home and heat them in the microwave before consumption.

Indeed, these factory-made ready-to-eat packs are significantly distinct from the traditional Tamil concept of a food parcel. While the former prioritizes quick convenience over the taste and nutritional value of the food, the latter encapsulates the rich culinary heritage and cultural traditions of the Tamil people.

For example, the meal is traditionally wrapped in banana leaves and consists of vegetarian curries accompanying the main dish. When placing an order, the name of the main curry dish is used. If it's chicken, you'd order a chicken curry meal, and if it's fish, it's a fish curry meal. Typically, the meal includes rice along with the main curry (which could be mutton, chicken, prawn, or fish) and several other vegetable curries, all wrapped together. When steaming hot rice and curries are wrapped in banana leaves, they absorb a unique aroma from the leaf. Upon unwrapping the package, you'll instantly notice this distinctive fragrance.

Moreover, upon receiving the food parcel, it introduces an element of surprise. You won't know which complementing vegetable curries are included until you open the pack and begin your meal. This element of surprise is one of the reasons why food parcels are highly appreciated among the Tamils. The post-chilli era snacks, often referred to as 'short eats,' are also highly popular among the Tamils. In the recipe section, you'll find a list of these 'short eats' that emerged during the Curry Renaissance. These curry snacks can be a delightful addition to your family gatherings and entertain your guests.

Sukku Coffee (Dry Ginger Coffee)

Before the British introduced tea to the Tamils, coffee was their first introduction, brought from the Arab world. However, it was quite bitter. As was customary, Tamils transformed it into a healthier beverage by incorporating herbs. In Tamil, 'sukku' refers to dried ginger.

Combining dried ginger, coriander seeds (another herb), and coffee beans created a perfect Tamil drink, adhering to the age-old adage that "food is medicine, and medicine is food." These ingredients are dark-roasted before being ground into a powder.

Traditional Tamil remedy for ailments like heartburn and indigestion, passed down through generations by Tamil grandmothers.

It's a fundamental element in every Tamil kitchen.

Ravi Maniam

And Finally!

We have covered a lot and thank you for travelling with me and also back into the history to explore the world of the Tamils and their curry heritage. Yet, after discovering the various challenges that curry lovers face and discussing the essential components of a potential solution, the crucial question remains: what practical steps can be taken moving forward?

This question is of particular importance for policymakers, restaurants, supermarkets and pub chains, media and individuals seeking to reclaim their love for curry. Let me take each group in turn in a moment. Because, by taking concrete actions and implementing policies that prioritise food safety, sustainability, encourage transparent labelling, and promote awareness and education, we can collectively work towards a future where everyone can enjoy delicious and safe curry without any health concerns.

Okay! Here are my practical recommendations for each group.

For restaurant owners:

Let's establish a standard so that customers can consistently know what to expect on their plate. We want customers to eagerly return for a memorable curry experience. As mentioned earlier, a customer ordering a Big Mac at McDonald's can anticipate the same taste whether in Bangkok or Glasgow. However, we are aware that this is not the case with curry. So now that we have a better understanding of what constitutes authentic curry, let's work towards setting a standard to safeguard the curry industry from potential challenges. This book is my contribution to this effort, following extensive research.

1. The vegan and vegetarian sector is big now, and yet curry is largely thought of as a non-vegetarian food. This perception needs to be changed and restaurant owners make sure to serve vegetarian curries and dishes as well.

2. Restaurants should aim to consistently offer curry according to a common standard rather than leaving it to individual chef interpretation, as we've seen in the case of Mulligatawny soup. This will ensure that customers can enjoy the same quality and flavors, regardless of where they choose to dine. Such standardization is essential for curry to thrive as a successful corporate business.

3. It's important to recognize that blaming the government for not issuing enough visas won't solve the challenges we're facing. Instead, we need to focus on addressing the issues within our own industry and working together to bring about positive changes.

It's of utmost importance to recognise that without addressing the concerns of both the government and our customers regarding curry, taking essential corrective actions, and gaining their support, we run the risk of losing our market share to emerging competitors in this highly competitive marketplace.

The Supermarkets, Coffee and Pub chains:

1. Supermarkets and pub chains that sell or serve curry to the nation should acknowledge their responsibility in supporting the curry industry during its challenging times. With a substantial market value of

approximately £5 billion, this is not an issue that can be overlooked any longer. Knowing what constitutes authentic curry now, it's the right thing to do to help curry lovers experience the real thing.

2. Keep in mind that curry encompasses more than just non-vegetarian dishes like Rice and Chicken Tikka Masala or Rice and Chicken Korma, which often contain preservatives. In today's era, customers are well-informed and have higher expectations, demanding authenticity in their food. Therefore, it's imperative to reassess and make necessary changes to the current situation. This book offers a multitude of healthy options to explore, including vegetarian choice.

3. As evident in the book, terms like "Indian Curry" and "British Curry" are insufficient to convince customers seeking authenticity. This issue has contributed to the "Curry Crisis," and it's essential to acknowledge it and take corrective measures to restore curry, the nation's favorite meal, to its rightful prominence it once enjoyed. It's also important to understand that the confusion surrounding the curry is a result of the overlooked 300 years history of curry with Portuguese and Dutch influence that predates the British era.

4. Furthermore, I would like to emphasize that coffee houses serving sugary and cheesy foods should also take action, especially considering that governments are intensifying efforts to combat excess sugar

consumption. These establishments should consider offering snacks or 'short eats' inspired by the Portuguese and Dutch era cuisine in Tamil culture.

The policy makers:

The government should help the curry industry by providing leadership and guidance and also ensure that the nation is consuming healthy and safe curry. The UK curry sector's turnover of about £5 billion is very big in term of tax revenue so the industry shouldn't be neglected and once it comes out of this current crisis, the market should be expanded – and thereby the revenue too.

The concept of the Curry Training Centre had good intentions but began without a proper study, resulting in its failure. The government should reconsider this initiative with the ideas highlighted in this book taken into account.

The purpose of Parliamentary Curry Group of 2015 should be clearly defined and reactivated in order for the group to look into the curry crisis and possible solutions.

(House of Commons - Register Of All-Party Parliamentary Groups as at 30 July 2015 : Curry Catering Industry)

The Media:

The media, particularly through television and newspapers, actively promoted various curry recipes via books and shows, adding to the existing confusion. It's now our shared responsibility to address this confusion and collaborate to revive and expand the curry industry, with the support of both the government and the public.

And last, my recommendations for the curry lovers:

I hope your search for the right sort of curry is coming to an end, and that by now you will also want to support the efforts of the curry industry to come out of the current crisis and prosper.

Certainly, I would recommend to everyone to use the five hundred year old Tamil – Portuguese innovation of Curry Thuool™ that comes originally from my village which, as you now know, was the first Portuguese exclusive Tamil colony before, later on, changing hands: first to the Dutch and then, finally, to the British.

Keep in mind that Sri Lanka and India were both founded by British colonialism, and both have areas which are the traditional habitats to the Tamil people, for whom the curry has been a staple dish for more than 3,000 years.

Focusing solely on India is not enough to complete the research on curry. The use of world's very first and authentic **Tamil -Portuguese Curry Thuool™** (Curry Powder) will allow you to savor the truly authentic curry of the post-chilli era and participate in the renaissance of Tamil curry, influenced by European culinary traditions.

It's important to remember that preparing curry is a simple, inexpensive process.

Finally, can I add one other important plea?

I remember, a couple of years back, the London Times newspaper publishing an article, titled, 'Let's stop children heading to an early grave', which pointed out the dangers of junk and processed food.

So, for the sake of your own health and that of our children, please say 'no' to processed meat and food. Instead, opt for fresh meat and take the time to prepare delicious food, maybe even a Tamil Curry!

A meme that has gone viral online

While this joke is timeless, it conveys a very clear message to us:

"I'm sorry to inform you that your blood pressure is slightly above the normal range and that your blood sugar is elevated, too" the doctor said to the young patient after the examination. I'll be writing you a prescription to take on a regular basis."

"Doctor, are there any side effects associated with the medication?" the patient asked, clearly worried.

"That's a question you should have posed to the bosses of businesses that sold you those junk food" said the visibly annoyed doctor. The patient, feeling a bit embarrassed, walked away, picking up the prescription.

The Great British Curry Renaissance

The time is ripe for a Curry Renaissance in the UK. Customers have patiently waited a revival, but their patience won't last forever. In a market that's fiercely competitive for new entrants, it would be unwise to let go of the foundation that was built through the immense hard work of many.

In today's internet era, customers are well-informed and have high expectations for quality experiences. It's important to acknowledge this reality and get ready for a significant transformation in the curry industry.

The curry industry owes a debt of gratitude to

Bangladeshi restaurants for their role in keeping it active, but they are in desperate need of assistance. Let's rally together to support them and address the challenges faced by all participants in the industry. Together let's work for a Curry Renaissance in the United Kingdom.

The Recipes

You may wonder why there are no recipes in this book. I've chosen a distinctive approach compared to other books. After considering feedback and comments that suggested including recipes could detract from the book's focus, I've decided not to include them in this volume. Recipes can sometimes be cumbersome to read, and they may not make much sense unless you're in the kitchen ready to follow and prepare the dish. As a result, I've chosen to present them through videos instead.

For access to my recipe videos, please visit my website at www.thatscurry.com. You'll find all the details there.

In these videos, whenever possible, we will embark on a journey to Tamil villages, primarily in India and Sri Lanka, as well as other locations. Our goal is to explore the diverse array of curries in these regions. We'll have the opportunity to meet the local people, immerse ourselves in their lifestyles, hear their stories, and, most importantly, discover their cherished recipes. Whenever the opportunity arises, we'll also share the food we prepare with the less fortunate in these communities. By watching these videos, you'll not only gain culinary skills but also contribute positively to the world.

I'd like to add one more thought. When it comes to providing for those in need, it can be a challenging task to offer something that truly satisfies. The human mind often craves more, whether it's in the form of wealth, knowledge, or material possessions. Nevertheless, there exists one thing in this world that can evoke the words "enough, no more" from someone - that is food. You can continuously fill a plate with food as someone is eating, and eventually, they will genuinely declare, "I'm full!" They can't pretend otherwise. This underscores the profound satisfaction and comfort that food can bring, making it a remarkable gift for those in need.

This is precisely why ancient Tamil literature advises us to feed the hungry, and we should heed this wisdom. By offering food to those in need, we can bestow upon them a gift that brings true satisfaction and, in return, experience the joy of giving.

APPENDIX 1

Ancient Tamil literature in which black pepper and curry were mentioned.

1. அகநானூறு : The Akananuru

The Akananuru, literally "four hundred poems sometimes called Nedunthokai (an anthology of long poems)", is a classical Tamil poetic work and one of the Eight Anthologies (Ettuthokai) in the Sangam period literature. According to Kamil Zvelebil (A Czech republic citizen) – a Tamil literature and history scholar, they are "one of the most valuable collections" from ancient Tamil history.

The Akananuru Poems - 149:

சுள்ளிஅம் பேரியாற்று வெண் நுரை கலங்க,
யவனர் தந்த வினை மாண் நன் கலம்
பொன்னொடு வந்து கறியொடு பெயரும்

Translation:

The 'Periyaru' (great river), also known as the 'Sulliyaru', flows through the country of Chera.

The Yavanas (Greeks and or Romans) drove large wooden vessels of strong structure, sails (from the Arabian sea) into the river Sulliyaru to stir the foam in it.

They brought gold in it and barter curry (pepper) and the trade took place at the harbour of Muciri.

2. புறநானூறு : The Purananuru

The Purananuru, literally "four hundred poems", is a classical Tamil poetic work and traditionally the last of the Eight Anthologies (Ettuthokai) in the Sangam period literature.

The Purananuru is the most important Tamil corpus of Sangam era courtly poems, and it has been a source of information on the political and social history of ancient Tamil Nadu.

According to Hart and Heifetz, the Purananuru provides a view of Tamil society before large-scale Indo-Aryan influences affected it. The life of the Tamils of this era revolved around the kindness.

Ravi Maniam

The Purananuru Poems – 168

அருவி ஆர்க்குங் கழைபயில் நனந்தலைக்
கறிவளர் அடுக்கத்து மலரந்த காந்தள்
கொழுங்கிழங்கு மிளிரக் கிண்டிக், கிளையொடு,
கடுங்கண் கேழல் உழுத பூழி,
நன்னாள் வருபதம் நோக்கிக், குறவர்
உழாஅது வித்திய பருஉக்குரற் சிறுதினை
முந்துவிளை யாணர் நாள்புதிது உண்மார்,
மரையான் கறந்த நுரைகொள் தீம்பால்,
மான்தடி புழுக்கிய புலவுநாறு குழிசி
வான்கேழ் இரும்புடை கழாஅது, ஏற்றிச்,
சாந்த விறகின் உவித்த புன்கம்,
கூதளங் கவினிய குளவி முன்றில்,
செழுங்கோள் வாழை அகல்இலைப் பகுக்கும்

Explanation:

அருவி பாயும் மூங்கில்-காடு. அந்த மூங்கிலில் மிளகுக் கொடிகள் படர்ந்திருக்கும். காட்டுப் பன்றிக் குடும்பம் அங்குள்ள காந்தள் கிழங்குகளைக் கிண்டி உண்ணும். அவை கிண்டிய புழுதியில் அங்கு வாழும் குறவர்- மக்கள் தினையை உழாமலேயே விதைப்பர். அதில் விளைந்த தினையை மரையான் என்னும் காட்டுப்பசுக்கள் மேயும்.

அந்த மரையானின் பாலைக் கறந்து ஊற்றி மான்கறியை அதில் ஊற்றிப் புன்கம் (பொங்கல்) சமைப்பர். சந்தன விறகில் தீ மூட்டிச் சமைப்பர். அவர்களின் வீட்டு முற்றத்தில் கூதளம்பூ பூத்துக் கிடக்கும். வரும் விருந்தினர்களுக்கெல்லாம் வாழை இலையில் அந்த முற்றத்தில் பங்கிட்டுத் தருவர்.

Curry heritage of the Tamils
Translation: Translated by George L. III Hart

Mountain which no one mounts, where hunters of the hills planted the tiny thick-sheathed millet, without any need to plow on a wide slope grown with bamboo as a waterfall roars, as pepper plants grow where the dry earth was plowed up by a family of boars so that the rich tubers of flowering kantal.

The hunters harvest the fresh growth (millet) so that they may eat well. They pour sweet foaming milk from a wild cow into and they set the pot on the fire.

Then, in the open, where it is lovely with wild jasmine and nightshade flowers, they eat their rice cooked with venison over sandalwood branches, sharing it out on the wide leaves of plantain trees that grow dense clusters of fruits!.

A. The Purananuru Poems – 343

மீன் நொடுத்து நெல் குவைஇ
மிசை யம்பியின் மனைமறுக் குந்து!
மனைக் கவைஇய கறிமூ டையால்.
கலிச் சும்மைய கரைகலக் குறுந்து
கலந் தந்த பொற் பரிசம்
கழித் தொணியான் கரைசேர்க் குந்து;

Explanation:

மீனை நிரப்பிக்கொண்டு ஆற்றில் செல்லும் அம்பி நெல்லை நிரப்பிக்கொண்டு வீடு திரும்பும். வீட்டில் இருக்கும் மிளகு மூட்டைகள் அந்த அம்பியில் கடற்கரைக்குக் கொண்டு செல்லப்படும். கப்பல் கலங்களில் கொண்டுவரப்பட்ட பொன் கழியில்

செல்லும் தோணியால் கரைக்குக்
கொண்டுவரப்படும்.

Translation: Translated by George L. III Hart

In Muciri with its drums, where the ocean roars, where the paddy traded for fish and stacked high on the boats that return to houses. Then the same boat loaded up with the sacks of curry (pepper) and traveled to a tumultuous shore where the golden wares brought by the ships bartered and were carried to land in the same boats.

3. ஐங்குறுநூறு: The Ainkurunuru

Ainkurunuru is a classical Tamil poetic work and traditionally the third of the eight anthologies (Ettuthokai) in the Sangam literature. According to Martha Selby, the love poems in Ainkurunuru are generally dated from about the late 2nd to 3rd century CE (Sangam period).

According to Takanobu Takahashi – a Tamil literature scholar, these poems were likely composed between 300 and 350 CE based on the linguistic evidence, while Kamil Zvelebil – another Tamil literature scholar – suggests the Ainkurunuru poems were composed by 210 CE, with some of the poems dated to 10 BCE.

The Ingurunuru Poems - 243

கறி வளர் சிலம்பின் கடவுள் பேணி
அறியா வேலன் வெறி எனக் கூறும்
அது மனம் கொள்குவை அனை, இவள்
புது மலர் மழைக்கண் புலம்பிய நோய்க்கே.

Explanation:

மிளகுக்கொடி வளர்ந்திலருக்கும் மலையின் தெய்வமாகிய முருகனை வாழ்த்திய பின்னர் வேலன் "வெறி" என்று கூறுகிறான். அதன் உண்மைத் தன்மையை மனத்தில் எண்ணிப் பார். புதிய மலர் போன்ற கண்ணை உடைய இவளுக்கு வந்திருக்கும் நோய் அது அன்று.

Translation:

Mother! Greeting: Murugan, the god of the mountain where the curry (pepper) grows, you agree that Velan, who is unaware of her disease caused by her fresh flower-like wet eyes, tears a lot, should be told that it was because of him.

4. குறுந்தொகை : The Kuruntokai

Kuruntokai is a classical Tamil poetic work and is traditionally the second of the Eight Anthologies (Ettuthokai) in Sangam literature. This short collection belongs to the akam (love) category.

A. The Kuruntokai Poems – 90

எற்றோ வாழி தோழி முற்றுபு
கறிவளர் அடுக்கத் திரவின் முழங்கிய
மங்குல் மாமழை வீழ்ந்தெனப் பொங்குமயிர்க்
கலைதொட இழுக்கிய பூநாறு பலவுக்கனி
வரையிழி அருவி உண்துறைத் தரூஉம்
குன்ற நாடன் கேண்மை
மென்தோள் சாய்த்துஞ் சால்பீன் றன்றே.

Explanation:

தோழி ! நீ வாழ்க ! மிளகுக்கொடி வளர்கின்ற மலைப்பக்கத்தில், இரவில் கரிய மேகம் முழக்கத்தோடு பெரிய மழையைப் பெய்ததால், மிகுந்த மயிரையுடைய ஆண் கருங்குரங்கு தீண்டியதால் நழுவிய, பூ போன்ற மணத்தை வீசும் பலாப்பழத்தை, மலைப்பக்கத்தில் விழும் அருவி, நீருண்ணுந் துறைக்குக் கொண்டுவருகின்ற குன்றுகள் உள்ள நாட்டையுடைய தலைவனது நட்பு, உன் மெல்லிய தோள்களை மெலியச் செய்தாலும், அமைதியைத் தந்தது ! இஃது எத்தகையது!

Translation:

Maid-friend hints about the heroine character to her lover who is waiting away for her.

There was thundering rain in the overlapping mountain where the curry (pepper) plant grows, at night time.

A jackfruit fell from its branch when a male monkey touched it. It was flown by the flood and floated in the waterfall's pond smelling fragrant even in its decaying stage.

B. The Kuruntokai Poem – 288

கறிவளர் அடுக்கத் தாங்கண் முறியருந்து
குரங்கொருங் கிருக்கும் பெருங்க னாடன்
இனிய னாகலி னினைத்தி னியன்ற
இன்னா மையினு மினிதோ
இனிதெனப் படூஉம் புத்தே ணாடே.

Explanation:

தோழி! மிளகுக் கொடி வளர்கின்ற
மலைப்பக்கத்தில், தளிரை உண்ணுகின்ற
குரங்குகள் ஒன்றாகத் திரண்டு இருக்கும் பெரிய

மலைகளையுடைய நாட்டின் தலைவன்,
பழகுவதற்கு இனிமையானவன். ஆதலின்,
சுற்றத்தார்களால் ஏற்படும் துன்பத்தைக்
காட்டிலும், இன்பம் நிறைந்தது என்று
சொல்லப்படும் தேவருலகம்,
இனிமையுடையதாகுமோ?

Translation:

The heroine says to her friend-maid:

He is a man of the mountain where the family of monkeys eats tender leaves of curry (pepper) creeper.

You; my friend, you say that he is kind. It is not true. Our relatives are pinning us connecting him with us. It makes me happy for me. They are speaking about our relationship. This speaking bliss is better than the bliss enjoying in the other world of heaven.

5. மதுரைக்காஞ்சி : The Mathuraik-kanchi

Maduraikanchi (Tamil: மதுரைக் காஞ்சி), is an ancient Tamil poem in the Sangam literature. It is a didactic poem and its title connotes the "poetic counsel addressed to the king of Madurai". Composed by Mankuti Marutanar – probably the chief court poet of the Pandya king Nedunjeliyan II, the Madurai-kanchi is the sixth poem in the Pattuppaattu anthology. The poem is generally dated to the late classical period (2nd to 4th century CE).

A. Mathuraik-kanchi Poem- 290

நறுங்காழ் கொன்று கோட்டின் வித்திய
குறுங்கதிர்த் தோரை நெடுங்கா லையவி

யைவன வெண்ணெலொ டரில்கொள்பு நீடி
யிஞ்சி மஞ்சட் பைங்கறி பிறவும்
பல்வேறு தாரமொடு கல்லகத் தீண்டித்...

Explanation:

குறிஞ்சி நிலத்துப் பயிர் - நல்ல வயிரம் பாய்ந்த மரங்களை வெட்டி வீழ்த்தி அவற்றைச் சுட்டெரித்த நிலத்தில் பயிர் செய்தனர். குச்சியால் குழி போட்டு அதில் ஊன்றிய தோரையின் (துவரை) குறுங்கதிர் விளைந்திருந்தது. ஐயவி என்னும் வெண்சிறுகடுகுப் பயிர் நீண்டு விளைந்திருந்தது. ஐவன வெண்ணெல் முற்றி விளைந்திருந்தது. இஞ்சி, மஞ்சள், கீரைவகைகள் முதலான பிறவும் பயன்படு தாரமாக (விளைச்சல் வருவாயாக) விளைந்த தானியங்கள் மலைப்பாறையில் கொட்டிக் காயவைக்கப்பட்டிருந்தன.

Translation:

Ample of grains were stretched out to dry on the cliffs; there was black pepper, turmeric, ginger, and small-eared thōrai paddy, produced on high ground where sandalwood and akil trees were cut off and burned. There was also white mustard with long stems that intertwined themselves in white mountain rice.

6. பட்டினப்பாலை : The Pattinappalai

Pattinappalai (பட்டினப்பாலை) is a Tamil poem in ancient Sangam literature. It contains 301 lines, of which 296 lines are about the port city of Kaveripattinam, the early Chola kingdom, and the Chola king Karikalan. The Pattinappalai describes the harbour capital city of the ancient Cholas, Kaveripattinam, and Chola kingdoms. The poem is an important and rich source of historical information about the ancient Chola kingdom and its capital city and its richness. It contains a vivid description of a busy maritime coastal city, the big ships, the fishermen, the markets, its festivals and feasts, and the people.

Pattinappalai Poem - 186

Wealthy streets of Kavirippoom-pattinam
பூம்புகாரின் செல்வ வளம் நிறைந்த வீதிகள்

The borders of the city with great fame are protected by the celestials. Swift horses with lifted heads arrive on ships from abroad, sacks of black pepper arrive from inland by wagons pulled by oxen, gold comes from northern mountains, sandalwood, and akil. wood comes from the western mountains, and materials come from the Ganges.

Pearls come from the southern ocean and coral comes from the eastern ocean. The yields of river Kaviri, things from Eelam, products made in Burma, and many rare and big things are piled up together on the wide streets, bending the land under."

7. மலைபடுகடாம்: The Malaipadukadam

Malaipaṭukaṭām is an ancient Tamil poem in the Pattuppaattu anthology of the Sangam literature. The poem describes the nature scenes, the people, and the culture of the mountain countryside under king Nannan. The poem is dated approximately 210 CE.

A few lines in the Malaipatukatam mention the shepherds, the fishermen, and the farmers along the Cheyyar River. The women in these regions state the poem and sing songs as they pound and husk the grains.

Malaipadukadam Poem Line 521

கருங்கொடி மிளகின் காய்த்துணர்ப் பசுங்கறி ...

Translation:

"Cluster of green peppercorns..."

***

I can give more historical detail about pre-chilli trades of the Tamils with the Europeans, Mesapothomyars, Babylonians, Egypt, and even with natives of New Zealand: The Maori people with whom a copper bell was found with Tamil inscriptions.

However, I reserve it for another occasion.

- Note that the researchers and translators mentioned here are all foreigners.

- Pattinam in Tamil means: a Town (Eg: Kaveri-Poom-Pattinam and Madarasi-Pattinam (Madras - Chennai now) where East India Company settled first on the Coromandel Coast.)

Appendix 2

The Europeans who travelled to the Tamils to spread Christianity and became proficient in Tamil language.

One of them, Henrique Henriques, a Portuguese Jesuit priest and missionary who lived from 1520 to 1600, was also known as Anrique Anriquez and spent the majority of his life working as a missionary in South India. After a few years in Goa, he relocated to Tamil Nadu, where he spent time learning the language and writing books, including a dictionary. He is regarded as the first Tamil scholar from Europe.

He firmly thought that religious doctrine books should be written in the native tongue, and as a result, he wrote books in Tamil. Tamil became the first non-European language to be printed in movable type thanks to his efforts. He is sometimes referred to as The Father of the Tamil Press as a result. Once he passed away, his mortal remains were interred in the Our Lady of Snows Church in Tuticorin, India.

Two books he printed and published. Both are about Christianity.

Another of the best European Tamil scholars, Father Beschi, translated the Tamil 'Thirukkural' into Latin about the year 1730 AD. To continue his missionary work in India, Rev. Beschi, an Italian Christian missionary, studied Tamil grammar and literature.

He adopted the Tamil name Veeramamunivar and dressed like a sadhu in saffron garments. He wrote the epic poem Thembavani, which tells the tale of Jesus Christ.

Beschi also published a grammar treatise titled 'Thonnool' and a prabandham titled 'Kavalur Kalambagam'.

One of the best children's stories features a Paramartha Guru (teacher) who isn't very brilliant and his much less intelligent students. Children still enjoy it.*(Paramartha Guru and his disciples)*

George Uglow Pope (24 April 1820 – 11 February 1908), or G.U.Pope, was an Anglican Christian missionary and Tamil scholar who spent 40 years in Tamil Nadu and translated many Tamil texts into English. His popular translations included those of the Tirukkural and Thiruvasagam.

Curry heritage of the Tamils

He later took to teaching, running his own school in Ootacamund for a while and then moving to head the Bishop Cotton Boys' School in Bangalore and after returning to England worked as a Lecturer at Balliol College, Oxford. A statue on the Chennai (Madras) beach recognizes him for his contribution to the understanding and promotion of the Tamil language.

'Thirukkural', a book about 'the Art of Living', is becoming more and more popular. It is made up of a thousand three hundred and thirty couplets called Kurals, each of which is an epigram that is both simple and alluring.

Thiruvalluvar, the creator of this magnificent art, lived between the third and the first century B.C. Tamil Nadu had extensive international connections throughout this time with nations like Egypt, Greece, and Rome in the west and Burma, Malaysia, and China in the east.

According to Strabo, a Greek who published his Geography in the first century AD, a delegation of the Pandya King attended the crowning of Emperor Augustus in Rome.

Another British born missionary and educator who opened religious schools in Northern Ceylon and South India during the British colonial era was Peter Percival (24July 1803 – 11 July 1882)

During his stay in Jaffna, Percival led the effort to translate the Authorized King James Version of Bible into the Tamil language, working with the Tamil scholar Arumuka Navalar – a Saiva Hindu. Percival's work influenced Robert Bruce Foote.

Percival began his career in British held Ceylon and Bengal (Calcutta was then British India's capital) as a Wesleyan Methodist missionary. He was instrumental in starting and upgrading a number of Christian schools within the Jaffna peninsula. After returning to England, he converted to Anglicanism.

Subsequent to his posting in South India, he severed his association with the Anglican Missionary Society that had sent him to India and worked as ane ducator in Presidency College in Madras Presidency.

Percival published English-Tamil and English-Telugu dictionaries as well as a number of books on Indian culture and religion. He died in 1882 in Yercaud in present-day Tamil Nadu.

Miron Winslow (11 December 1789 – 22 October 1864) was an American Board of Commissioners for Foreign Missions missionary to the American Ceylon Mission, Ceylon (now Sri Lanka), where he established a mission at Oodooville and founded a seminary. He founded a mission station at Madras, the first and chief station of the American Madras Mission. Harriet Winslow, his wife, also served as a missionary alongside and wrote a memoir thereof.

He published several books, notably, A History of Missions and A Comprehensive Tamil and English Dictionary of High and Low Tamil, a Tamil to English lexicon which took twenty years of missionary labor to compile sixty-seven thousand Tamil words!

This dictionary was based in part on manuscript material of the pastor Joseph Knight, of the London Missionary Society, and the Rev. Samuel Hutchings, of the American mission, and was the most complete dictionary of a modern Indian language published at that time. The book later become the basis for the more exhaustive Tamil Lexicon dictionary published by the University of Madras in 1924.

Prof. Dr. Kamil Vaclav Zvelebil was born in Prague (Czechoslovakia) whose impact to the knowledge of Tamil literature, particularly in the west, cannot be overstated.

He proved much of what we now take for granted, such as the fact that Tamil literature truly was a national literature with its own unique traits, forms, and techniques, much like French or German literature. He was also instrumental for gaining widespread support in the West for the early dating of Sangam literature, correctly.

Additionally, Professor Zvelebil showed how Tamil literature was cohesive as a whole. He demonstrated how, common threads permeated Tamil literary genres throughout its history, whether they were single stanzas, "short poetical works", epics, or devotional poetry.

His Lexicon of Tamil Literature will continue to be the go-to resource for ideas, works, and authors in Tamil literature for the foreseeable future due to the enormous range of his expertise.

Appendix 3

The cultural remnants of the Europeans

The Portuguese era had a profound and enduring impact on Tamil food culture, particularly in the transformation of curry. The introduction of chili and various new vegetables played a significant role in reshaping culinary traditions. Additionally, the advent of wheat flour and the bakery tradition marked a culinary milestone, leading to the widespread popularity of bread as a breakfast choice. Many individuals now relish the combination of bread with red lentil curry and coconut sambal, making it a preferred choice.

Like Congee, bread has become a staple for low-income families who may not afford a more elaborate meal based on rice and curries.

Portuguese Love cake and Dutch LumpRice and Rick Cake remain popular to this day. Many delicacies, particularly snacks (short eats) from the Portuguese and Dutch periods, are still popular and widely served for all occasions on the island and even among the diaspora.

Despite the Portuguese leaving Sri Lanka 365 years ago, the native Kaffringha dance has survived to this day because to the descendants who still reside there. Even the local men are familiar with the Portuguese Kaffringha Dance. Baila music, originating from Portuguese traditions, is popular in Sri Lanka.

Numerous Portuguese words, such as Mesai (Table), Janel (window), Sapato ('Sapaththu' - shoe), camisa (Shirt), and armário ('Alumari' - Cupboard), as well as the Dutch word Kamar (Room), have been incorporated into the Tamil language. In certain rural villages, these words are still used in their original form because the items they refer to were relatively new introductions to Tamil culture, and thus they've been retained, even as English became more prominent. Recall that quite a few Tamil words can be found in both English and European languages.

It's fascinating to see how languages evolve and adapt through cultural interactions. Borrowed words from other languages, often become integrated into the local language and are used in various contexts.

Curry saw a revival during the Portuguese era that persisted until the Dutch era - both for about 300 long years.

The Tamil region received a proper legal framework during the Dutch era. The Dutch introduced tobacco cultivation, and it continues to be grown in various regions, including my village, the entire islet, and in the Jaffna peninsula.

However, the strongest footprint is that of the British. British legacies include the English language, judiciary, schooling, universities, railroads, bridges, and many other structures.

No one speaks Portuguese or Dutch, but the English language is still around and became an important language and continues to be widely spoken and used in business, education, and government and doesn't seem to be disappearing any time soon.

The British promoted Western-style education in India and Ceylon, leading to the establishment of universities and schools. This had a significant impact on both countries intellectual and academic traditions.

Complex Legacy: The British legacy is a subject of ongoing debate. While it brought certain benefits and modernization, it also left behind a legacy of exploitation and cultural complexities that continue to shape identity and trajectory of both India and Ceylon.

The British legacy is a multifaceted and often controversial topic, and its impact continues to be studied and discussed by historians and scholars.

***

The Tamil - Portuguese Curry Thuool™ (Curry Powder)

Just to recap, in the early 16th century, the Portuguese captured the Tamil islets surrounding the Bay of Mannar to secure the sea area famous for pearl fishing. Their arrival introduced Chilli and 130 new vegetables to the region, sparking a culinary transformation known as the 'Curry Renaissance.'

The world's first Tamil curry powder, born from the fusion of Tamil and Portuguese influences, originated from these islets 500 years ago. This closely guarded recipe has been handed down through generations, with many attempting to replicate it in vain. One such effort was 'Madras Curry Powder,' which is not popular or known in Madras (Chennai). All indications point to consumers being misled when the authentic producers failed to respond. While it might be unrealistic to expect the Portuguese to rectify this situation, the Tamils have the capacity to do so.

To conclude, let's do what we haven't done so far!

This book pays tribute to both Christopher Columbus and Vasco Da Gama for their great contribution to the curry heritage of the Tamils.

In his second vogue, the former brought chillis from South America to Europe, and the latter brought it from Europe to the Tamils of the spice island, who up until that moment had been using black pepper for their curries (pre-chilli era).

| Christopher Columbus | Vasco Da Gama |

Following the introduction of chilli and at least a hundred and thirty new plants and vegetables to the Tamils by the Portuguese, the post-Chilli era began, which is when the Curry Renaissance started taking place.

*****

For any communitcation: www.thatscurry.com

www.ingramcontent.com/pod-product-compliance
Lightning Source LLC
Chambersburg PA
CBHW030110100526
44591CB00009B/351